Usability Assessment of Library-Related Web Sites

Methods and Case Studies

edited by
Nicole Campbell

Guide #7

a division of the **AmericanLibraryAssociation**
Chicago and London

ISBN 0-8389-8157-7

Printed in the United States of America

05 04 03 02 01   5 4 3 2 1

Over the past six years, librarians have spent an ever-increasing amount of time developing and maintaining library Web sites. These Web sites have become the primary gateways to library resources, including online catalogs, databases, electronic journals, research guides and many other library services. As libraries become ever more dependent on their Web sites, however, it is important to question whether users can actually use these sites successfully, whether they can find what they are looking for, or whether they get frustrated and decide to look elsewhere for help. One way to find out whether a web site is useful and usable is to conduct a usability study of the site.

There are many articles and books that describe usability methods and discuss how to conduct usability studies. Many of these are listed in the "Selected Web Sites and Readings" section at the end of this text. The purpose of this Guide is to focus specifically on library-related Web sites. It is designed to provide libraries and librarians with basic information about usability assessment as well as examples of how other libraries are assessing usability of their Web sites.

Chapter 1 defines the concept of usability and provides a synopsis of methods for measuring usability. Chapter 2 discusses some of the important elements to consider when conducting a usability study. The remaining chapters provide a practical look at usability assessment. These chapters, or case studies, are examples of actual usability studies that have been done by a variety of libraries, including public and college libraries. They cover a variety of usability methods, but all focus on assessing library-related Web sites.

Nicole Campbell

chapter 1

Usability Methods

Nicole Campbell

Defining Usability

Usability is defined by the International Standards Organization (ISO) as the "extent to which a product can be used by specified users to achieve specified goals with effectiveness, efficiency and satisfaction in a specified context of use" (ISO 1998, p. 8). In general, usability looks at how a user interacts with a system or product as they perform basic tasks. The focus is on users and whether they can successfully use the system or Web site.

In addition to this basic definition, there are often important attributes or factors linked with the concept of usability. These attributes help determine the usability of a product and can often be used to measure that usability. As an example, the ISO definition of usability includes four attributes: effectiveness, efficiency, satisfaction and context of use. *Effectiveness* looks at whether users can accomplish tasks completely and accurately. *Efficiency* analyzes the amount of resources used to complete tasks effectively. *Satisfaction* deals with a user's attitude towards the product. Finally, *context of use* looks at the specifics of the social and physical environment in which the product is used (ISO 1998, p. 8). These four attributes serve as metrics for determining a product's usability.[1]

Usability has its roots in computer science and engineering, most directly with the field of user-centered design. User-centered design has gone under many names over the years, including human-computer interaction, ergonomics, human factors and usability engineering. It is a process of designing usable products and systems "so that users can perform required use, operation, service, and supportive tasks with a minimum of stress and maximum of efficiency" (Rubin 1994, p. 10). User-centered design has three main principles. First, it puts a focus on users and tasks early in the design process by continually gathering information about users, their needs and how they would use a product. Second, it emphasizes measuring product usage, primarily ease of use and learnability, through testing. Third, user-centered design emphasizes iterative design, where a product is designed, tested, modified and retested continually.

1

Based on these principles, usability is an important aspect of good user-centered design because measuring usability focuses on users and user tasks, tests product usage, and is an integral part of an iterative design process.

table 1. Definitions of the Eight Methods Included in This Text.

Methods for Measuring Usability

There are many methods for measuring a system's usability. This text does not describe every method as there are many good articles and books that already do this.[2] There are eight methods, shown in Table 1, described in this text. These methods are the most commonly used and they work well for testing Web sites. Many of these methods are also discussed in more detail in the case studies.

In general, there are two types of methods for assessing usability. One type uses real users for gathering information. The other type uses the site designers or experts. The methods discussed below that use actual users are usability testing, card sorting, category membership expectation, questionnaires or surveys, and focus groups. The methods included here that do not involve actual users are cognitive walkthrough, site usage logs, and heuristic evaluation.

Usability Testing

The phrase "usability testing" can be confusing because it is often used to describe the entire process of measuring or assessing usability, regardless of which method is used. However, the phrase originates from one particular method for measuring usability. Often called formal usability testing, this method involves having participants perform tasks using the system or Web site being tested, or using paper prototypes of the site. As participants complete the tasks, they are often asked to verbalize their thoughts, reac-

---

Usability Testing - A method that tests how a user interacts with a system. The participant is given a list of pre-defined tasks to accomplish using the system and asked to "think out loud" about their thoughts, reactions and feelings.

Card Sort - A method for testing the structure of a web site or application using index cards, each representing an individual concept or web page. Participants arrange the cards in an order or structure that makes sense to them.

Category Membership Expectation - A method that tests the participants' understanding of various categories including what they think should be in each category and what the category should be named.

Focus Groups - A method that involves a small group of individuals discussing their opinions and ideas about a defined topic or set of topics.

Questionnaire - A set of questions designed to collect responses and opinions from users on a topic.

Analysis of Site Usage Logs - A method of using web server (httpd) logs to track users' movements on a web site. This is especially useful for determining patterns of movement and use.

Cognitive Walkthrough - Designers of the web site or product try to predict users' movements and actions by doing actual tasks themselves.

Heuristic Evaluation - A group of evaluators analyze the interface of a "system" based on a set of usability principles, called the heuristics.

table 1. Definitions of the Eight Methods Included in this Text.

2

table 2. Example Tasks for Formal Usability Testing

tions and feelings out loud. Test observers monitor this process, recording any comments and whether the participant succeeded or failed at each task. The purpose of this method is to analyze the participants' reactions and behavior while using the system.

The most crucial part of doing formal usability testing is creating the list of tasks that participants will complete using the Web site or system. These tasks should be representative of actual things average users would do on the site. For instance, a task might be "What are the library's hours?" Table 2 shows some example tasks.

When creating tasks it is important to pay special attention to the wording of each question and use words that are not leading or biased in some way. People will often look for keywords on the Web site that relate to keywords in the task. Sometimes, this is appropriate but other times, this will inadvertently skew the results. The best advice is to take special care when constructing tasks and then test them out on someone else, such as a colleague, faculty member or friend, before conducting the real test.

It is also important to limit the number of tasks based upon the amount of time allotted for test sessions. For instance, giving a participant a list of forty-five questions to complete in one hour will be overwhelming and exhausting for them. Plus, it will be difficult for participants to actually finish all the tasks within the given time. On the other hand, giving participants ten to fifteen questions still provides valuable feedback and is a less overwhelming experience. The key here is to be focused and create tasks based on the study's objectives, which are the specific things being measured by the study. (Objectives are discussed further in Chapter 2.)

Determining the number of participants to include in a formal usability test is an interesting issue. There is generally no universal rule on how many participants need to be used in formal usability testing and, as with all usability methods, there really cannot be too many participants. However, research has shown that using four or five test participants will reveal eighty percent of the usability problems with a system that would be retrieved even when more users are tested (Rubin 1994; Nielsen 2000). Jakob Nielsen, a well-published usability expert, notes that "the best results come from testing no more

3

Example Tasks

Does the library have access to a database called Medline?   ___Yes   ___No

Is Medline available from home?   ___Yes   ___No

Locate the page that lists Internet resources. What is one of the recommended search engines?   _____

Imagine that you have found a book that you would like to order from another library. Is there information on how to order books through interlibrary loan?   ___Yes   ___No

Locate a list of databases for History.

Find the directions for how to access library resources from home.

table 2. Example Tasks for Formal Usability Testing

than 5 users and running as many small tests as you can afford as part of an iterative design process " (Nielsen 2000, paragraph 1).

figure 1. Sample Index Cards for the Card Sort

One thing to consider when deciding upon the total number of participants is whether there are many distinct groups in the user population. For instance, at a university, distinct groups would include faculty, graduate and undergraduate students and staff. For distinct groups that may use a system differently, it is recommended to test three to four users from each category of user (Nielsen 2000, paragraph 10). This means that a formal usability test can be conducted with only five participants, although the total will probably be closer to eight or ten people, depending on how many distinct groups are represented in the user population.

Finally, it is important to note that conducing formal usability tests can actually be a very simple process. In some places, elaborate laboratories are used for conducting tests. These laboratories have extensive video recording systems and include observation rooms for onlookers. In contrast with this, it is also possible to conduct these tests in a simple manner. It really only requires sitting down at a computer with a participant and a list of tasks. Observers can make comments on paper. The real cost is usually the time involved in designing and conducting the tests.

Library Homepage

Internet Resources

figure 1. Sample Index Cards for the Card Sort

Card Sort

This method tests the structure or organization of a Web site or system. To do this, index cards are labeled with individual concepts, menu items or, in the case of a Web site, names for individual web pages, as shown in the examples in Figure 1. Blank index cards are provided in case a participant wants to place an item in more than one category. During the test, participants are given the index cards and asked to arrange them into categories or groups that make sense to them, labeling any categories or piles they have created. Participants then take the groups they have created, organize them into groups or categories, and then label these new groups. Participants are encouraged to ask questions about anything that is confusing to them. Observers are present to answer any questions and to record any comments and reactions made by the participant.

The card sort is useful because it shows what items or Web pages users place together. For instance, participants may place the "Library Hours" card in the same group as the "Directions to the Library" card or they may place the "Library Databases" card in the same group as the "Help Documentation" card. The card sort also provides

table 3. Instrument for the Category Membership Expectation

a look at the vocabulary that participants use in labeling their categories. This is particularly useful given the jargon that is often used in libraries and on library systems. The card sort can show, for example, whether participants use the word "circulation" or if they prefer words like "borrowing" or "checking items out."

Analyzing the results of the card sort can be tricky. The results can be analyzed statistically using what is called a cluster analysis, which looks at the relationships between card groups. Statistical software packages, such as SPSS or SAS, can help with this type of analysis. On the other hand, it is also possible to simply scan the results, looking for trends and patterns. Scanning the results will not provide the level of detail available from a cluster analysis, but is a useful method for getting quick results or for people who are not statisticians. Regardless of which method is used for data analysis, the results are directly dependent on the total number of participants used because there is so much variability in how a single participant may group their cards. With a small group of participants, it is very easy for one participant's results to skew the final results. However, as the number of participants increases, it is much easier to notice patterns and trends.

Category Membership Expectation

The category membership expectation is designed to test participants' understanding of categories and their labels. To do this, an instrument is created that lists each individual Web page on a site and provides extra blank space, as the example in Table 3

Category Membership Expectation

Participant #_____ Date: _____

Here is a list of categories on the Library's web pages. Please note what kinds of material you would expect to find under each of these categories. You do not need to limit yourself to the space that is provided – use as much room as you would like including the back of pages. If you think that a category should be given a different name please tell us what you think it should be called.

Name of Category	Contents of Category (What you would expect to find)	Suggested Name for the Category
Library Services	_____	__ _____
	_____	
	_____	
	_____	
Circulation	_____	__ _____
	_____	
	_____	
	_____	

table 3. Instrument for the Category Membership Expectation

table 4. Sample Questions for a Focus Group

shows. Participants are asked to describe what they would expect to find under each of these Web pages or categories. For example, given the category of "library resources" a participant may say that she expects to find databases, ordering forms, the library catalog, and Internet resources. Then, participants are given the opportunity to rename this Web page if they desire.

The category membership expectation is a good method for looking at vocabulary, as is true of the card sort method. This method, though, is particularly useful because it focuses directly on how categories or Web pages are labeled and what participants think those labels mean. It is a highly focused method. In addition, the results are easy to analyze by scanning the instruments for any themes, patterns or trends.

The major drawback of this method is that it can be exhausting for the participants because they are writing out feedback for each category. This is especially true if there are a large number of Web pages or categories. For instance, a small Web site may have twenty or more categories. One way to help alleviate this problem is to test only a portion of the entire Web site at a time or to divide the categories up amongst groups of participants. For instance, in a study with eight participants, four participants could be tested with half of the categories and four could be tested with the other half.

Focus Groups

Focus groups are a common research method, used in many disciplines. Libraries use them for a variety of purposes, including user studies and library assessment studies. In this method, a group of participants are gathered together to discuss their opinions and ideas about a defined topic or set of topics. This discussion is directed by a moderator and is often monitored by several observers. Usually, the discussion in recorded. To help direct the conversation, moderator's use a set of questions that help focus

---

Focus Group Questions

Start with everyone answering question #1.

Describe your experience with the library's Web site.

What do you use most regularly on the site?

Can you find what you need easily?

Is there anything that you have tried to find (or expected to find) and couldn't?

What do you think about the layout and design of the site?

What about the vocabulary used on the site? Do all the words make sense to you?

What is your overall opinion of the site?

Are there any other comments you would like to make?

table 4. Sample Questions for a Focus Group

---

on the topics being studied. Table 4 shows some example questions for a focus group on usability.

There are some useful tips to consider when using focus groups for usability studies. During the discussion, it is helpful to provide participants with screen shots or some sort of visual display of the Web site being tested. This gives participants a visual reminder of the site and helps to focus the discussion. Also, the moderator should be someone unaffiliated with the research being conducted. This helps eliminate any bias the researchers may lend to the conversation and allows the researchers to act as the observers.

Questionnaires

Questionnaires are a set of questions designed to collect responses and opinions from users. This commonly used research method can be given in a variety of formats, including Web-based forms and mail-in forms, to a large number of people and can be designed for a variety of purposes. For instance, a short questionnaire could be used to get demographic information about participants or to ask how often they use the library's Web page. Questionnaires, like the sample shown in Table 5, work well in conjunction with other methods. For example, participants can fill out an exit questionnaire after they have completed one of the other methods.

As a whole, questionnaires are easy to analyze. Open-ended questions can be scanned for trends, problems and themes. Questions that use pre-defined answers, such as likert scales, can usually be analyzed statistically. Consequently, questionnaires can be given to large numbers of people without greatly increasing the amount of effort needed to analyze the data.

Analysis of Site Usage Logs

Web servers keep a variety of logs files. The format depends on the type of server and how that server is configured. Most servers are set up to record every request received, including web pages and images. For instance, every time someone looks at a library's homepage, the server records a request for the homepage itself and every image on that page. This means that log files can get very large. Some servers are also configured to save search logs, which record every search done on the site with the site's search engine.

Initially, log files can seem confusing. However, there are some standard elements included in these files. As an example, Table 6 shows sample log entries from a Netscape Web server. In this example, each line represents an individual request. The name of the computer making the request is listed first, followed by the date and time of the request and then the specific item being requested, such as "library.html" or "lib.jpg". Other types of servers may include slightly different information.

Log files can be used for a variety of purposes, but are especially useful for showing patterns of use and movement. For instance, they can show which pages on a site are requested continually and which pages are rarely accessed. They can also show

7

table 5. Sample Questionnaire

which days and times most people use the site. Search logs can show what types of things users are trying to find and what language they use to locate these things. However, logs do not reveal if users are successful in finding what they need on the site. They also do not show what a user's reactions, opinions or emotions are when using the site. Logs can help with looking at the usage of a site but really should be used in conjunction with other methods when analyzing the usability of a site.

Because log files are extremely large, it is impossible to thoroughly analyze them manually. However, there are many software packages available to help. These packages process the logs and generate statistical reports about site usage. Choosing which analysis software to use depends on many factors including the type of logs being examined and the amount of resources a library wants to spend on software.

Questionnaire

Participant # _____ Date: _____

Please answer the following questions about how you use the library's Web site. Thank you for your time.

How often do you use the Library's Web site:

__ Never used it
__ Once or twice a semester
__ Once or twice a month
__ Once or twice a week
__ Daily

Overall, the Web site seems easy to use. (Check one).

__ Strongly Agree
__ Agree
__ Neither Agree or Disagree
__ Disagree
__ Strongly Disagree

Where do you access the Web site from?
(Mark as many as appropriate.)

__ In the Library
__ In the Computer Lab
__ Elsewhere on campus
__ From Home
__ Other

What is the best feature(s) of the site?

_____
_____
_____

What is the worst feature(s) of the site?

_____
_____
_____

If you selected "Other", please describe:

_____
_____

table 5. Sample Questionnaire

Cognitive Walkthrough

Also called a design walkthrough, this method involves having designers or other experts complete tasks using the Web site instead of using real users. Before they

table 6. Entries from a Web
Server Log File

begin, participants are given a list of tasks similar to those used for a formal usability test. While completing the tasks, participants try to predict how real users would do things on the site. Observers monitor the process and note any problem areas or concerns.

This method is particularly useful in the early stages of a Web site design because it can be done before the site is fully developed or even with paper prototypes of the site. This is especially useful for highlighting possible problem areas before the site is fully developed. Walkthroughs can be done quickly and cheaply because participants are people who are already working on the design and development of the site.

The biggest disadvantage of this method, however, lies in the fact that it uses designers rather than actual users. The designers are trying to guess or envision what users might do with the site. While this works to some degree, designers behave and think differently than average users, especially inexperienced users. Designers also have the benefit, and the bias, of personal experience with the design and organization of the site. For this reason, cognitive walkthroughs can never be a replacement for getting feedback from real users.

Sample Log File

c935402-a.vncvr1.wa.home.com - -[01/Oct/2000:00:24:04 -0700] "GET /vis/lib/library.html HTTP/1.1" 200 -

c935402-a.vncvr1.wa.home.com - -[01/Oct/2000:00:24:11 -0700] "GET /vis/lib/db/1p-trans.gif HTTP/1.1" 200 43

c935402-a.vncvr1.wa.home.com - -[01/Oct/2000:00:24:04 -0700] "GET /vis/lib/WSUVmain3.jpg HTTP/1.1" 200 7457

c935402-a.vncvr1.wa.home.com - -[01/Oct/2000:00:24:11 -0700] "GET /vis/lib/db/WSUVresources2.jpg HTTP/1.1" 200 7323

c935402-a.vncvr1.wa.home.com - -[01/Oct/2000:00:24:11 -0700] "GET /vis/lib/db/new.gif HTTP/1.1" 200 165

c935402-a.vncvr1.wa.home.com - -[01/Oct/2000:00:24:04 -0700] "GET /vis/lib/1p-trans.gif HTTP/1.1" 200 43

c935402-a.vncvr1.wa.home.com - -[01/Oct/2000:00:24:04 -0700] "GET /vis/lib/new.gif HTTP/1.1" 200 165

c935402-a.vncvr1.wa.home.com - -[01/Oct/2000:00:24:11 -0700] "GET /vis/lib/db/alldbs2.html HTTP/1.1" 200 -

table 6. Entries from a Web Server Log File

Heuristic Evaluation

Heuristic evaluation is another method that involves designers instead of real users. This method uses a set of usability guidelines, called heuristics. Like the examples shown in Table 7, heuristics are based on recognized usability principles.[3] For instance, a heuristic may look at the help and documentation available on the site or may focus on the consistency of language and design. Using the heuristics, a group of evaluators analyze the Web site to determine problem areas. After the evaluators analyze the site individually, the results are compiled into one list of usability problems.

In the computer science field, evaluators are normally usability experts. However, this method could be accomplished using the Web site designers, librarians or library staff. The total number of evaluators to use with this method is fairly flexible; however using more than one evaluator will help ensure that more usability problems are noticed. It has been shown that single evaluators will only notice 35% of the usability problems with a system (Nielsen 1993, p. 156). As a whole, the number of evaluators will vary depending on the specific situation. However, having three to five evaluators seems reasonable (Nielsen 1993, p. 156) and is a manageable number.

table 7. Sample Heuristics

Sample Heuristics

Be consistent with language and design throughout the site.

Use language that makes sense to users.

Provide help documentation.

Make sure the site is accessible to all types of users and browsers.

table 7. Sample Heuristics

WORKS CITED

ISO 9241-11. Ergonomic requirements for office work with visual display terminals (VDTs)–Part 11: Guidance on usability. London: International Standards Organization, 1998.

Nielsen, Jakob. Ten Usability Heuristics. http://www.useit.com/papers/heuristic/heuristic_list.html, Accessed 12/3/00.

Nielsen, Jakob. Usability Engineering. Boston: Academic Press, 1993.

Nielsen, Jakob. "Why You Only Need to Test With 5 Users." Jakob Nielsen's Alertbox, March 19, 2000. http://www.useit.com/alertbox/20000319.html, Accessed 12/2/00.

Rubin, Jeffrey. Handbook of Usability Testing. New York: John Wiley & Sons, Inc., 1994.

FOOTNOTES

1. For other examples of usability attributes, see Jakob Nielsen's *Usability Engineering*, p. 26-27 and Jeffrey Rubin's *Handbook of Usability Testing*, p. 18-19.
2. The Suggested Readings at the end of this text include many useful texts on different usability assessment methods.
3. See, for example, Jakob Nielsen's "Ten Usability Heuristics" at http://www.useit.com/papers/heuristic/heuristic_list.html.

chapter 2

Conducting a Usability Study

Nicole Campbell

Important Aspects of Conducting a Usability Study

- ▼ Creating a Purpose Statement and Objectives
- ▼ Selecting Methods and Developing Instruments & Scripts
- ▼ Conducting a Preliminary Test
- ▼ Selecting and Recruiting Participants
- ▼ Conducting the Usability Study
- ▼ Analyzing and Implementing the Results
- ▼ Some Final Suggestions

There are, of course, many different ways of conducting a usability study. The specific steps will vary depending on the specifics of each situation, organization and library. This section is not designed as a list of required steps. Rather, this is intended to highlight some important aspects, outlined in the sidebar, that can help make the process of conducting a study go more smoothly.

Creating a Purpose Statement and Objectives

One of the most important, and early, steps in a usability study is to develop a purpose statement and a set of objectives, like the examples shown in Table 1. The purpose statement explains why the study is being done and is usually a broad concept, similar to a goal. For instance, a sample purpose statement might be "to determine if library patrons can use the library's Web site effectively to conduct their research." In contrast, the objectives are more focused statements that describe the specific activities or questions that are going to be tested. As an example, an objective could be "Can users find the library's address and contact information?" Both the purpose statement and the objectives provide focus and guidance throughout the testing process and are especially helpful when choosing test methods and designing instruments.

Selecting Methods and Developing Instruments and Scripts

Based on the study's purpose and objectives, it is relatively simple to select test methods. For example, if the study is looking at a Web site's vocabulary, it might be useful to use the card sort or category membership expectation methods. On the other hand, if a study is looking at how people use a site, a formal usability test or even

table 1. Examples of Purpose Statement and Objectives

table 2. Sample Script

Purpose Statement

Does the current organization of the library's Web site make it possible for library users to easily locate what they need?

Objectives

- ▼ Can users find the "Resources by Subject" section of the site?
- ▼ Can faculty find the "Faculty Resources" Web page?
- ▼ Can users located the help documentation?

table 1. Examples of Purpose Statement and Objectives

questionnaires may work best. Often, using multiple methods provides more thorough feedback. One common way to do this is to use questionnaires in conjunction with other methods because the predefined questions on a questionnaire balance nicely with the feedback from other methods. Choosing test methods will also depend on the timeline for the study and the resources available.

In addition, it is important to develop scripts for the study. Scripts, like the example shown in Table 2, provide instructions and information about the test and are read before each test session. Using a script ensures that each test participant hears exactly the same information before they begin. They also provide consistency throughout the usability study.

Finally, because usability studies involve humans as test participants, it may be necessary to have test materials reviewed by a human subjects panel or board. A

Introduction to the Study Script

Hello. My name is ____ and this is ____. We are going to be working with you in today's session. We are glad that you have volunteered to help us assess our library's Web pages. Your contribution will be very valuable.

We have been using the Web to explain and provide library services for more than two years and we want to know how it is working for people and what we can do to make it better. One part of this is to figure out how best to organize all the information on the library's Web site. This is what you will be helping us with today. We want you to know that YOU are not being tested. How you complete a task will not reflect on your skills. We are testing the organization of our Web pages, not you.

During today's session, we will give you a series of tasks to do using cards, which represent individual web pages, services or policies. Arrange these cards into categories or groups that make sense to you. During the session, we will be taking notes and watching what you do. Just ignore us—we will not be commenting on your skills but will just be recording what you do.

It is okay to ask questions during the session. We may not be able to answer them, but it is okay to ask. Do you have any questions before we begin?

table 2. Sample Script

human subjects review analyzes whether the study treats participants ethically and with care. This helps to ensure that participants are not harmed in any way while they are participating. This review is not necessary at every library or institution, and is usually only necessary at colleges or universities. Research or grant personnel or other librarians that have done research with human participants will know if such a review is necessary.

Conducting a Preliminary Test

Conducting a preliminary test is a useful way of working out any bugs in the study. Preliminary, or pilot, tests use the actual test instruments and are conducted in the same manner as the real test. They can be done with one or two participants. These participants can be anyone, including library staff, student employees or even friends. These preliminary sessions often reveal some usability problems but, more importantly, they catch problems with test instruments or procedures.

Selecting and Recruiting Participants

The process of determining how many and what type of participants to include in a usability study is ultimately dependent on the methods used and the individual library environment. However, there are some general guidelines that can prove useful. The most important thing is to try to select people who are representative of the library's user population. At a university, for instance, this would include graduate and undergraduate students, faculty and staff. If the total number of test participants is going to be small, it is best to choose participants that are representative of the average user rather than people who represent only small subgroups of users (Nielsen 1993, p. 175). This will ensure that the results are representative of average users. With larger numbers of test participants, try to select participants who represent various subgroups within the user population.

Selecting people with a variety of skill levels is enlightening as well. This is especially true of users who have very little experience with the Web site or even with computers or the Internet. These novice users will often use a Web site differently and consequently, will reveal different usability issues than those users who are more experienced. Using a questionnaire that asks questions about demographic and computer experience can help with the process of selecting participants from different user populations and with different skill levels.

Recruiting people to volunteer for a study can be done in many ways, again dependent on the individual library environment. Advertising is a useful tool; this can be done in a variety of ways including over email listservs, newsletters or newspapers, word of mouth, or even posting signs around the community. Providing an incentive of some sort also helps with recruitment. Incentives generate interest in volunteering and act as a reward or compensation for people who do participate. Incentives can be a variety of things, ranging from money or prizes to copy cards or gift certificates.

Conducting the Usability Study

The process of conducting the actual tests is relatively straightforward and depends greatly on which methods are used. For those methods that involve bringing in actual users, it is important to set up the test environment in as realistic and comfortable way as possible. This helps lessen any potential discomfort a participant may feel and also makes the test as natural as it can be. For methods that involve observers, it is useful to go over expectations before the tests begin. This includes what sorts of things the observers are looking for and recording and even where to sit so as to be able to view the test but not intimidate the participants.

With some methods, it is useful to record test sessions. This can be done using a variety of equipment, including tape recorders or camcorders and tripods. Try to place equipment so that it will be able to record everything accurately but is again not intimidating for the participants. Also, test the equipment before test sessions begin to make sure it is functioning properly.

After a test session is finished, it is beneficial for the observers to spend some time debriefing. This provides an opportunity to compare notes and discuss general reactions and opinions from the session. This will help ensure that everything is noted and discussed before any new data is collected.

Analyzing and Implementing the Results

Analyzing the results of a usability study varies from method to method. For many of the methods, it is possible to simply "eye-ball" the results to look for trends and problem areas. This can be done swiftly and easily. It is important, though, to have more than one person look at the results. This extra set of eyes helps to ensure important trends, problem areas and general observations are noticed.

The process of actually implementing the results of the usability study is probably one of the most difficult. Again, as with the other steps in conducting a study, this will vary from library to library. Some libraries have teams or committees involved in the design of Web sites, whereas others may only have a person or two. Because of this, the complexity of the implementation process is highly unique and variable.

However, there are two things that will help this process along. First, it is useful to establish a timeline for implementing any results. This keeps everyone on schedule and also helps ensure that changes are actually made to the site. Second, creating an action plan is a useful way to establish both a redesign outline and a workflow scheme. Action plans are simply a list of the problems that were discovered in the study along with solutions for each of these problems. Regardless of how this works out, implementing the results of the usability study is a vital part of the process for making a more usable site.

14

Some Final Suggestions

There are some important aspects to usability assessment that do not quite fit elsewhere in this chapter. First, usability studies can actually be quite inexpensive. Often, the biggest cost is the staff time spent in developing and conducting the test. In addition, there are always some minimum costs for incentives, equipment and supplies. Otherwise, usability studies can be done with very little cost to the library.

More importantly, the cost involved really is quite low when compared with the amount of valuable information collected from test participants. Usability studies provide libraries with an opportunity to create better services and to get to know more about their users. In the case of the formal usability test method, it also provides an opportunity to watch how participants actually use a Web site and browser. This is very enlightening for any reference or instruction librarian. For these reasons, usability studies are definitely worth their costs.

Finally, usability studies are a valuable part of the iterative design process. Libraries are spending so much time and energy creating Web-based resources that it is vital to make sure these resources are useful and usable. Measuring their usability is a method for doing this. It is also important to keep measuring usability with every redesign. This process brings users into the design process and makes libraries more user-focused.

chapter 3

Learning as We Go
Arizona State University West Library's Usability Experience
Kathleen Collins and José Aguiñaga

About ASU West Library

Arizona State University West (ASU West) is a commuter campus in west Phoenix, Arizona, with 5,000 enrolled students. We are part of the 3-campus Arizona State University system, located 25 miles to the west of the main campus in Tempe, Arizona. Since 1984, ASU West has been one of only a handful of upper-division universities in the United States, offering junior-, senior-, and master's-level courses. Starting in the Fall of 2001, however, the campus has added lower division undergraduate courses to its offerings.

The campus library emphasizes electronic access to information, and the library's web site is its primary information gateway. All of ASU West Library's web development is done in-house, directed by our 3-person Web Council and using the varied talents of existing staff.

What We Studied and Why

The Library's web site design had remained substantially unchanged since its debut three years ago, although it had grown from its original 34 pages to some 240 pages as the Library's services increasingly included web components. A design that had been workable in its original size began to show signs of wear, and reference staff reported that students had problems navigating the site. [**Figure 1** shows the original site in February 2000.] Finally, in the spring of 2000, the Library's Web Council, which is responsible for the overall management of the organization's web initiatives, charged two interdependent teams to completely redesign the web site by May. The Web Redesign Team developed five site prototypes. The Web Usability Team conducted a literature review, devised an instrument with which to evaluate the usability of various site

figure 1. ASU West
Library's Original Web Site

designs, and administered three rounds of task-oriented testing to a total of thirty-five students, staff and faculty. The redesign team then used data generated by each round of testing to eliminate some prototypes and refine the remaining sites. Both teams reported to the Chair of the Library's Web Council, and the Library's web master served on both teams and acted as a liaison between site design and usability testing activities. [**Table 1** depicts the relationship of the two teams to the overall web management of the Library; **Table 2** shows the inter-dependent timelines of both teams during the web redesign and usability testing projects.]

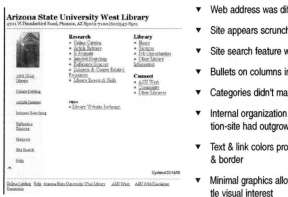

▼ Web address was difficult to remember

▼ Site appears scrunched to the top left

▼ Site search feature was de-emphasized

▼ Bullets on columns inhibited quick scanning

▼ Categories didn't make sense to Library users

▼ Internal organization of page made it difficult to locate information-site had outgrown the organization

▼ Text & link colors provided little contrast with page background & border

▼ Minimal graphics allowed pages to load quickly, but provided little visual interest

figure 1. ASU West Library's Original Web Site

17

Methodology of the ASU West Library Usability Testing

While the Redesign Team generated the five prototype site designs using the Dreamweaver web editor and Adobe PhotoShop, the Usability Team concentrated first on learning about web usability testing through a literature review and then on planning the study's design and execution. ASU West Library had never before undertaken formal usability studies, though some team members were familiar with usability concepts and methods. There was no shortage of good literature on usability design, but we found a shortage of materials on testing *library* web sites. We wanted concrete examples of library usability studies, complete with sample testing instruments and practical assessments of what worked. We found only three, from MIT (1999), Yale (Prown 1999), and University of Arizona libraries (1997), but they proved invaluable.

After reading up on various usability methods, the team decided to go with the *usability testing* methodology for various reasons. We felt that we weren't expert enough to perform heuristics or cognitive walkthroughs ourselves, and we wanted information about the look and feel of the site as well as its terminology and organization. We were looking for the unanticipated quirks and gut reactions that only our user

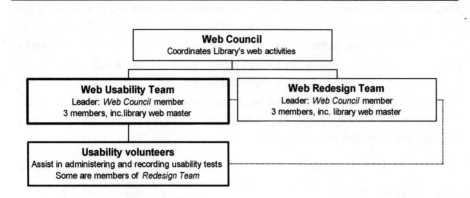

table 1. Structure of ASU West Library's Web Redesign

table 2. Usability Project Timeline

table 1. Structure of ASU West Library's Web Redesign

population could give us. As well, it made sense to involve students, faculty, and staff in the redesign process from a public-relations standpoint. Finally, many Library staff had recently participated in a series of student focus groups, so the team could draw on their experience with neutral questioning techniques for help in administering the actual testing. In short, this method seemed to be the most rewarding and manageable method, and the experience of observing users as they interacted with the different designs would be a valuable learning experience for staff.

Because the Redesign Team had constructed five site prototypes and was interested in employing usability data to narrow down the possibilities, we planned several iterative stages of testing. [**Table 3** describes the testing stages.] First, a pre-test of library staff would identify any problems with our testing instrument. Next, a paper prototyping phase would identify the top two designs. [**Figures 2 – 6** show the five paper pro-

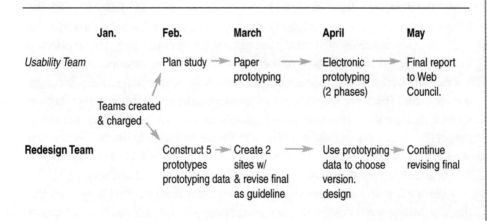

table 2. Usability Project Timeline

Sidebar 1: Usability Tasks

- ▼ Locate the place where you would go to find a book on genetics owned by ASU.
- ▼ Identify a source in which you could find an article on genetics.
- ▼ Locate the database entitled Art Index.
- ▼ What time does the library open on Sunday?
- ▼ Find information on ASU West Library services that are available to students with disabilities.
- ▼ Find a listing of Internet search engines.
- ▼ Find a list of all electronic journal titles owned by the ASU Libraries
- ▼ Find a guide listing resources on diversity topics
- ▼ Locate the online form for booking a video
- ▼ Find a guide on Internet resources available from the US Government

Note for questioners: After each question, ask each participant why s/he chooses a certain link or path

18

table 3. Stages of ASU
West's Usability Testing

totypes, with rankings and comments from the usability tests.] The Redesign Team could then use the data from the paper prototyping to develop two electronic prototypes, which would in turn be tested for their usability. [**Figures 7 and 8** show the two electronic prototypes, with rankings and comments.] Once the final site was identified, we planned one final round of tests in order to identify any remaining problems with the new site. [**Figure 9** shows the final site design after all usability testing was completed.] We allotted at least one week for each stage of testing, and one to two weeks between each stage to allow the Redesign Team time to assimilate usability feedback into the next generation of site prototypes. After each phase of usability testing was complete, the Usability Team compiled and summarized the testing data and sent a report to the Redesign Team.

Having settled on our methodology, the team next constructed a multi-layered testing instrument. First, we jointly identified tasks that library users commonly perform on our site, and then brainstormed questions to test whether people could complete those tasks using the Redesign Team's site prototypes. The team decided to prompt each participant to explain why they chose a particular link or followed a particular path—in effect, to think out loud while they attempted to complete each task. Because we were interested in comparing the various prototypes to see which ones the users preferred, we decided to ask each participant to look at all of the prototype designs.

Each participant

▼ completed tasks using each prototype (See **Sidebar 1**). We asked participants in the paper and electronic prototyping stages to complete 5 tasks for each prototype, varying the questions for each individual and presenting the questions and the prototypes in a different order each time. For the final design, participants completed all 10 tasks. Because participants were only given the home page designs in the paper prototyping stage and thus could not follow each task through to completion, we varied the task questions by prefacing them with "Where would you expect to find…"

Stage	Prototypes	Participants	Tasks	Debrief	Time	Prototype Images
Pretest of questions	3 paper s mock-up	3 library staff	10 per prototype	individual & comparative	1 hr.	Figs. 2–6
Paper prototyping	5 paper mock-ups	5 students & faculty	5 per prototype	individual & comparative	1.5 hr.	Figs. 2–6
Electronic prototyping	2 electronic sites	18 students & faculty	5 per prototype	individual & comparative	1 hr.	Figs. 7 & 8
Final design test	1 electronic site	12 students & faculty	10 per prototype	individual (extended)	1 hr.	Fig. 9

table 3. Stages of ASU West's Usability Testing

figure 2. The "Books" Paper
Prototype

Arizona State University West Library
4701 W. Thunderbird Road, Phoenix, AZ 85069-7100   (602)543-8501

| Online Catalog | Article Indexes | Internet Searching | How Do I | Site Search | ASUW |

- **Research and Reference**
  Catalog · Article Indexes · Internet Searching · Subjects Guides · More...

- **Course Related Information**
  Library Skills Tutorial · Reserves · Course Resources · More...

- **Library Services**
  Book Renewal · Patron Information · Requesting Material · Media Booking · More...

- **More About Us**
  What's New · Hours · Directories · Job Opportunities · More...

Comments   Updated 2/23/00

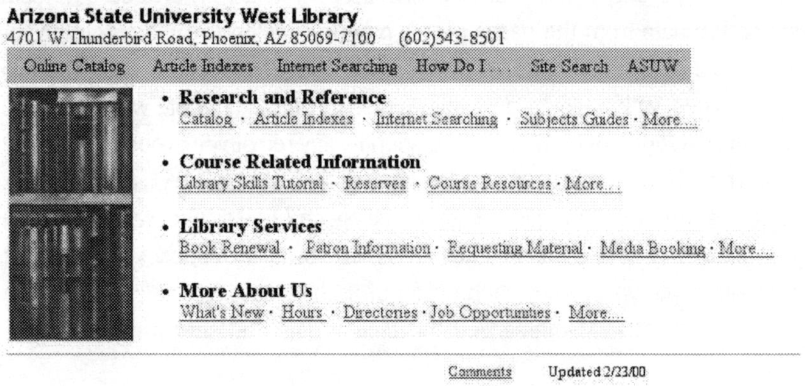

Rank: 1 out of 5   Ratings: Ease of use 3.6   Organization 3.8
1=difficult...5=easy   1=not effective...5=effective

- ▼ "This feels scrunched & cramped. Everything's crowded into the top. Use more white space."

- ▼ "I don't like the books, they seem like a cliché."

- ▼ "I like the books, they feel like a link to the past. They make me feel nostalgic."

- ▼ "I like this 'More...' at the end, it means you don't have to put everything on the first page."

- ▼ "I don't like 'More...', especially with the dots underlined. More what? Why not spell it out?"

figure 2. The "Books" Paper Prototype

- ▼ answered debrief questions about each prototype's organization, aesthetics, and vocabulary (See **Sidebar 2**). Much of our most valuable feedback came during this part of the testing.

- ▼ compared the prototypes and identified features of each that should be incorporated into a final design. We gave participants paper printouts of each design and asked them to rank them from best to worst, then to mark each printout up using pencils and colored dots (green for features they liked, red for ones they disliked). Participants suggested alternative vocabulary and placement, sketched graphics, drew arrows, crossed features out.

Usability Assessment of the Web Site

The testing was administered in an empty office in the Library, which was reserved for the duration of the usability testing for our exclusive use. We did our best to make it a non-threatening and informal environment by re-arranging furniture and decorating it with plants, colorful posters, and knick-knacks on loan from our colleagues. For the electronic phases of the testing, the Library's Technology Support and Development Department arranged for the loan of an iMac computer from our local Apple represen-

Sidebar 2: Debrief Questions

- ▼ Overall, finding specific information was: 1 2 3 4 5 (difficult—easy)

- ▼ What makes you rate it this way?

- ▼ Organization of our site was: 1 2 3 4 5 (not effective—very effective)

- ▼ What makes you rate it this way?

- ▼ As you were using this web site, what did you like? What worked well for you?

- ▼ Aesthetically what was pleasing? (Prompt for specifics: Text size, Ease of finding links, Colors, Graphics, Spacing, etc.)

- ▼ As you were using this web site, what didn't you like? What didn't work well for you?

- ▼ Aesthetically what was not pleasing? (Prompt for specifics: Text size, Ease of finding links, Colors, Graphics, Spacing, etc.)

- ▼ What would you change about this web site?

- ▼ (Hand testers a pencil and allow them to mark up a printout of the page with comments, arrows, drawings, etc. Prompt for specific vocabulary and anything they mentioned in the "didn't like" question.)

Figures 2–9 include average rankings and examples of comments made during the debriefs.

figure 3. The "Green" Paper
Prototype—Embedded

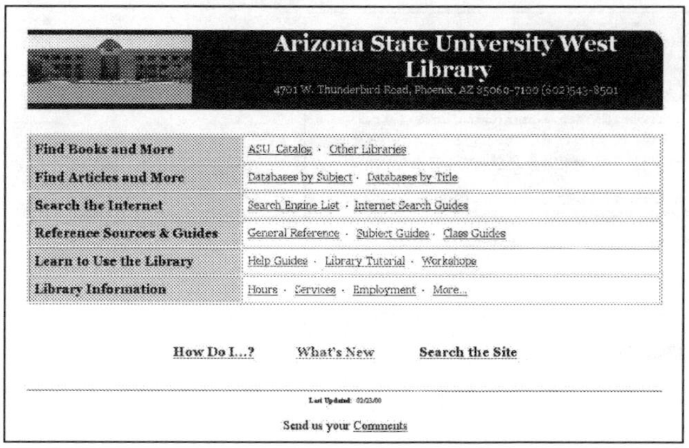

Rank: 2 out of 5*   **Ratings: Ease of use 3.6   Organization 3.4**
tied with "Blue"   **1=difficult...5=easy   1=not effective...5=effective**

▼ "The banner takes up too much of the page's real estate. It weighs the page down and gives it a forbidding air."

▼ "I like that the links are blue. I get confused as to what is a link and what isn't when they're another color."

▼ "Words are large & easy to read. There's lots of white space, & the organization lets me scan quickly."

▼ "Wording is easy to understand—'Find Books', 'Search the Internet.' I like the 'How Do I...? idea."

▼ "This grey color is blah. I would expect these headings to be clickable."

figure 3. The "Green" Paper Prototype—Embedded

tative. The computer was loaded with both the Netscape Navigator and Internet Explorer browsers, so that participants could use whichever program they preferred. Each test involved two Library staff: one to administer the test and guide participants through the process, and a second to record as completely as possible the participant's verbal and non-verbal reactions. Staff who volunteered as either test administrators or recorders were briefed on what to do (and what not to do) during the testing; many of our volunteers had moderated focus group interviews the previous fall, and were well-versed in neutral questioning techniques. In all, 12 library staff served as administrators and/or recorders during the usability testing, some of whom also served on either the Usability or Redesign teams.

Meanwhile, we had been working on lining up participants for the usability testing itself. Our recruitment of participants was, again, multi-layered. Because of the number of prototypes we had to test, we hoped to recruit at least 30 participants overall, 20 of which were to involve students and the remaining 10 faculty and staff. As anyone who works at a university knows, getting people to give up an hour or so of their time in the midst of a busy semester can be a challenging task at the best of times. To recruit faculty and staff, we sent out general emails, but also drew on our personal connections to particular individuals, calling in favors and promising ones in return. We had discov-

figure 4. The "Blue" Paper Prototype

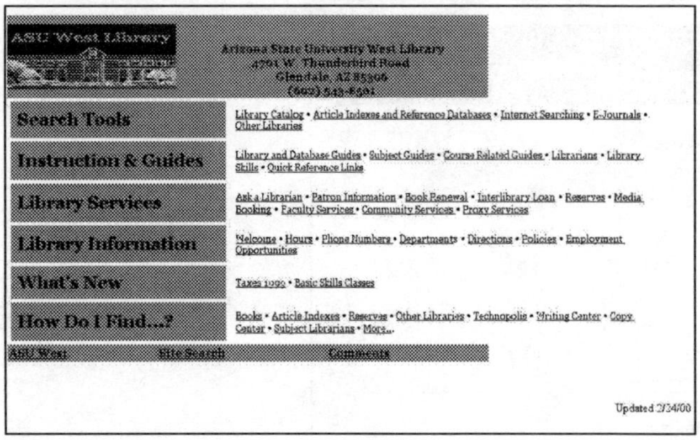

Rank: 2 out of 5*   **Ratings: Ease of use 4.2   Organization 4.2**
*tied with "Green"   1=difficult...5=easy   1=not effective...5=effective
prototype

Some reactions from testers:

▼ "What is Interlibrary Loan, Patron Information?

▼ What's the difference between Librarians, Subject Librarians, and Ask a Librarian?"

▼ "The picture makes the library look dark & forbidding."

▼ "The detail means I don't have to guess. I can find whatever I need by reading this page."

▼ "It's too dark, on top and left; it feels overbalanced."

▼ "There's too much detail. Words are so small that it's not easily to scan them. Use one fewer category."

▼ "I like that media booking and book renewal are right out here. "

▼ "Why isn't 'Welcome' the first thing, instead of being buried in the 4th category?"

figure 4. The "Blue" Paper Prototype

ered during focus groups held in the fall of 1999 that, for a non-residential campus whose students don't spend a lot of out-of-class time on campus, incentives are the key to student recruitment. As a state institution, ASU West Library is barred from giving cash compensation, but we are allowed to use one of our funds to provide campus goods and services. We settled on $10 certificates to the university bookstore for each student who participated in our study. We created a recruitment ad **[Figure 10]** and distributed it across campus, posted it on the Library's web site, published it in the student newspaper, and emailed it to students who had participated in the Library focus groups. In the end, we attracted 35 people (22 students, 6 faculty, and 7 campus staff) to participate in the usability study, including a member of the Disabilities Resource Center, who gave feedback on the accessibility of the electronic designs for users with print disabilities.

figure 5. The "Kokopelli" Paper Prototype

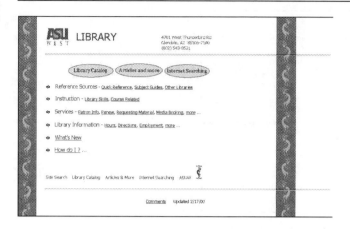

Rank: 4 out of 5   Ratings: Ease of use 3.6   Organization 3.4
                      1=difficult...5=easy   1=not effective...5=effective

Some reactions from testers:

▼ "This page feels unbalanced; all the weight goes toward the left."

▼ "I don't see the text at first. My eye is drawn only to these big yellow buttons."

▼ "You should have either text links or button links here, but not both."

▼ "The Kokopellis invoke the Southwest, but they're not from around Phoenix area, are they?"

▼ " The word "Library" and the address look like they've just been slapped on with one of those old rubber stamps."

▼ "There's not enough information on the first page. I'm left guessing where to click."

figure 5. The "Kokopelli" Paper Prototype

Usability Test Findings

At the end of each phase of the study, the Usability Team analyzed all the data generated by the testing. Each team member read all the transcripts of the individual tests and then the team held a meeting to identify common themes and uncommon problems for each prototype. We also calculated the average ratings that participants assigned for each prototype's ease of use and organization and their overall rankings. These numerical ratings reinforced our more subjective impressions, and we used them primarily as a double-check system to make sure our subjective impressions were on the right track.

After all the testing was done and the data analyzed, what did the ASU West Library team find out about library web site usability? Here are the main things that the team learned:

▼ Users think differently than librarians about the organization of information. While this seems obvious, the extent of this difference surprised us nonetheless, and participating in user testing was an important learning experience for library staff.

figure 6. The "Swoosh"
Paper Prototype

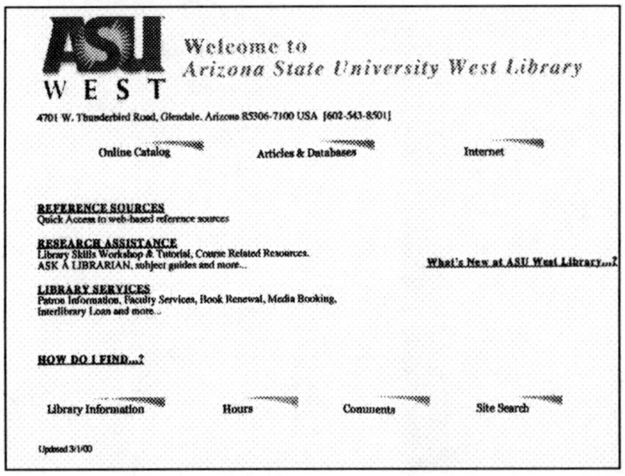

Rank: 5 out of 5   Ratings: Ease of use 2.4   Organization 2.4
1=difficult...5=easy   1=not effective...5=effective

Some reactions from testers:

▼ "It's hard to read the text under the headings in the middle area."

▼ "Are these supposed to be buttons? They don't really look like buttons."

▼ "The ASU West logo ties the library into the larger campus."

▼ "This page is trying to lead my eye in too many directions at once. It's just not scannable."

▼ "The page feels angry. There's too much red."

▼ "The links should be blue, not black. I can't tell what's a link here and what's just text."

▼ "I like that there's not much text on the page."

figure 6. The "Swoosh" Paper Prototype

Redesign Team members who served as usability recorders found the experience especially informative: "When you actually see someone interacting with a site you've designed it's different than reading a dry report, and the problems become obvious."

▼ The first reaction users had to a site was always to its "look and feel." Therefore, in site usability, intangibles like colors, images, font, and text size and placement can be as important as actual content. For instance, many of our participants expressed a strong preference for the standard blue links, and objected if they thought one of our prototypes was doing something that was not standard. Many participants also expressed a strong desire for a "sense of place" while using the site, in the form of pictures of the library building, familiar names, an address. We conclude that such a sense of place is an important comfort factor for users of a library web site.

▼ There's a fine line between too much text and too little, and testing helps tell you when you've crossed it.

figure 7. The "Blue" Electronic Prototype

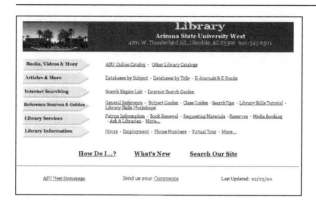

Rank: 1 out of 2   Ratings: Ease of use 4.1   Organization 4.4
1=difficult...5=easy   1=not effective...5=effective

Some reactions from testers:

▼ "The blue color is soothing, and it works with the blue links."

▼ "Those dots after 'More...' are annoying. You should spell it out—More What?"

▼ "I hate the title 'Library.' What's your actual name?"

▼ "The button that says 'Reference Sources & Guides' looks scrunched, and that heading seems sort of vague...what's a guide? Isn't the whole site a guide?"

▼ "The 4th and 5th lines look really crowded and are hard to read. Needs more white space, and maybe a larger font."

▼ "I really like those 3 big links at the bottom. They stand out, sound friendly but seem important."

▼ "These services should link to the actual online forms, not to 'how to' pages."

▼ "The term 'search engine list' is unclear. Do you mean for searching the Internet?"

▼ "The page is easy to scan, works with natural sightlines—down, then across."

▼ "Don't like the picture. It looks kind of forbidding. Why not just have a picture of the library building?"

figure 7. The "Blue" Electronic Prototype

▼ The wording you use is make-or-break—for example, the difference between "Online Catalog" and "Library Catalog" is small, but was important to our testers, who preferred the term "Library" in front of the word "Catalog" because there are other types of catalogs online. However, our participants didn't focus on specifics like wording until they had dealt with the "look and feel" of the interface.

▼ People who develop web pages need to pay special attention to the sight lines and scannability of their pages, and must test sites to see whether users can easily skim for information. Our users lost important contextual information in some of the page designs we tested, because their eyes jumped right over it. Additionally, sites must be easily read by the screen-reading programs that many people with visual disabilities use.

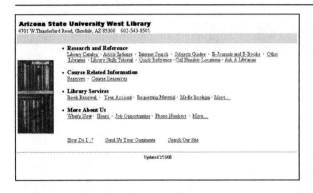

figure 8. The "Books" Electronic Prototype

Rank: 2 out of 2   Ratings: Ease of use 3.4   Organization 3.3
1=difficult...5=easy   1=not effective...5=effective

Some reactions from testers:

▼ "This doesn't scan well. My eyes have to go across, then return to the right and go across again."

▼ "I found myself ignoring the headings and only looking at the links underneath. So, the site organization was lost to me."

▼ "These books are so generic. The page doesn't convey a sense of place, other than that of a library, any library."

▼ "There's less information on this page [than Figure X], so I don't have to read so much."

▼ "The first section seems really crowded and is hard to read."

▼ "This site just seems a bit amateurish to me."

figure 8. The "Books" Electronic Prototype

▼ Library users have little perception of the "boundaries" between a library web site and the online catalog and subscription indexes. Moving from the controlled look of a web site into another interface disrupts the continuity of a user's search for information, and yet individual libraries exert little control over these outside interfaces.

▼ In order to be most effective, usability testing must be iterative and ongoing. ASU West Library began receiving feedback about what worked and what didn't work with our new site shortly after it debuted. In addition, the introduction of the campus's first lower-division classes in the Fall 2001 meant that the Library would be dealing with a new user population with new information needs. There is no such thing as a perfect site, and a design that is workable one year can be outgrown the next as technologies and people change.

▼ Our usability study suggested that there are most likely some gender, age, and cultural differences in the ways people interact with online information. Although we drew no firm conclusions about what those differences are, we will have to be careful to recruit different populations in our next round of testing to avoid a site that is biased toward one mode of interaction.

figure 9. ASU West
Library's New Web Site
(http://www.west.asu.edu/
library/)

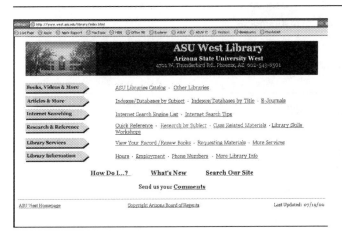

▼ Web address is streamlined

▼ Sight lines move down, then right, making the page easy for users to scan.

▼ Header conveys sense of solidity. Blue color tested well.

▼ All common library functions are described on the home page.

▼ Images convey information and add visual interest to the page.

▼ Links are the standard blue color, minimizing user confusion.

▼ Terminology is simple and user-tested.

figure 9. ASU West Library's New Web Site
(http://www.west.asu.edu/library/)

27

▼ Usability testing isn't just for web sites. We have expanded our usability testing efforts to areas beyond our web site, such as the interfaces for our new self-check machine and the ASU system's shared catalog.

Conclusions: ASU West's Experience with Usability Testing

Since this was a learning experience for ASU West Library, inevitably we would do things a bit differently were we to start over again. The Usability Team compiled a final report for the Library's Web Council at the end of the site redesign project. In it we recommended some things to keep and some to change:

▼ Start any web usability study by conducting usability tests for the existing site; some things may work well, and you will find out what does need to be changed.

▼ Give team members time to accommodate their learning curves. The frantic pace of our study, which took only three months to learn about, design, and administer three rounds of testing while the Redesign Team simultaneously generated prototype after prototype, didn't leave us much time to gear up.

figure 10. Flyer Used to
Recruit Participants in the
Usability Study

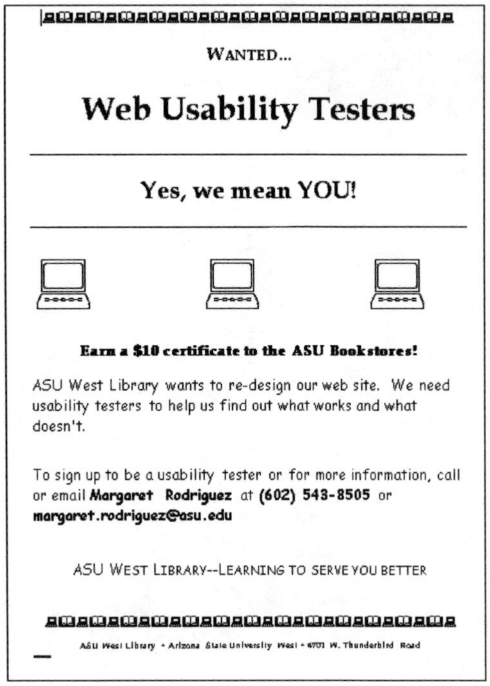

WANTED...

Web Usability Testers

Yes, we mean YOU!

Earn a $10 certificate to the ASU Bookstores!

ASU West Library wants to re-design our web site. We need
usability testers to help us find out what works and what
doesn't.

To sign up to be a usability tester or for more information, call
or email **Margaret Rodriguez** at **(602) 543-8505** or
margaret.rodriguez@asu.edu

ASU WEST LIBRARY--LEARNING TO SERVE YOU BETTER

ASU West Library • Arizona State University West • 4701 W. Thunderbird Road

figure 10. Flyer Used to Recruit Participants in the Usability Study

28

▼ Spend the time to pre-test and refine the questions you will ask your study participants, and pre-test on non-library personnel. A few of our questions had unin-
tentionally misleading vocabulary which could have been identified and corrected during a more thorough pre-test.

▼ Recruit more participants during the paper prototyping phase. This initial step in
the testing process turned out to be more useful than we had anticipated,
because we asked our five participants to compare all five prototypes and comment on their preferences. This testing stage helped the Redesign Team decide
which designs to further develop into prototype sites, and saved invaluable time.

▼ Retain the iterative stages of testing. Though the paper prototyping was useful,
the site our participants ranked at the top during this phase was not the top one
during the electronic prototyping. In the paper phase, people were torn between
the "Green" and "Blue" prototypes, and their split vote caused "Books" to rank
number one.

▼ Hold co-meetings between the design and usability teams at crucial points during the redesign.

▼ Perform some rapid-response development in the early stages of the testing,
using small batches of participants and using that feedback to identify and correct obvious problems.

▼ Test some external clients (those who are neither students, faculty, nor staff of the university) as a control group.

Our most conservative estimate is that our team spent 240 person-hours designing, conducting, and evaluating ASU West Library's Spring 2000 usability study: 160 hours to research, plan, and evaluate data, and 80 hours to conduct the testing and summarize the results. It was simultaneously an exhausting and gratifying endeavor, but when the Library's new user-friendly web site debuted in August 2000, the feedback we received from students made it all worthwhile.

WORKS CITED

Gordon, Seth. "User Testing: how to plan, execute, and report on a usability evaluation." CNET Builder.com, February 15, 2000. Available: http://www.builder.com/Graphics/Evaluation/

Massachusetts Institute of Technology. MIT Libraries Web Advisory Group. "Web Site Usability Test." (Documentation of usability studies conducted in March 1999). Available: http://macfadden.mit.edu:9500/webgroup/usability/results/

Prown, Sarah. "Detecting 'Broke': Usability Testing of Library Web Sites."
Yale University Library, 1999. Available: http://www.library.yale.edu/~prowns/nebic/nebictalk.html

University of Arizona Library. Access 2000 team page. (Includes presentations and documentation of usability studies conducted in 1997) Available: http://dizzy.library.arizona.edu/library/teams/access9798/

Arizona State University West Library: http://www.west.asu.edu/library/

chapter 4

Building a User-Centered E-Presence at the Auburn University Libraries

Robert H. McDonald

Background

The Auburn University Libraries are a part of Auburn University, Alabama's Land-Grant University. Located in Auburn, Alabama, the University provides 130 undergraduate, 64 master's, and 40 doctoral areas of study for more than 22,000 students. The libraries consist of the Ralph Brown Draughon Library, the Carey Veterinary Medical Library, and the Library of Architecture, Design and Construction. A member of the Association of Research Libraries and the Association of Southeastern Research Libraries, the Auburn University Libraries comprise the largest library in the state of Alabama.

An early adopter of Internet technology, the libraries had a Web server as early as 1993, and our Web presence, or e-presence, developed between 1993 and the present with only one major structural re-design. During the 1999-2000 academic year, our administration decided it was time that the libraries' Web presence had a new look. To accomplish this task, we convened a new committee of six library faculty and staff to both manage and build the new site look and structure.

This new committee, the AU Libraries' Web Advisory Group (hereafter referred to as the advisory group), decided to take this opportunity to not only re-design the look of the site but also to design a new information structure for our libraries e-presence. Using the usability and user-centered ideas of Jakob Nielsen, Jared Spool, and Clare-Marie Karat we were able to accomplish this task and stay within our deadline of 6 months to a new look and structure.

figure 1. Chart showing
target research groups
for our libraries' Web site.

The Study

In any major re-design project, a timetable is extremely valuable. In this instance our six-month deadline was probably a bit hasty. We were not only re-designing the look of the site but were also trying to build an information structure that would serve many different research populations. We wanted our homepage to be friendly to undergraduates but still enable faculty, staff, reference librarians, and virtual visitors to utilize the site.

Since we did not have a choice about our deadline the advisory group immediately worked out an outline in late 1999 to follow through the first 6 months of 2000 for re-designing and implementing our new site. This outline follows:

▼ January 2000 – Develop a re-design methodology - Why to re-design?
▼ February 2000 – Create paper and HTML rough draft prototypes – What to re-design?
▼ March 2000 – Test prototypes via focus groups, iterative surveys, and cognitive interviews – How to re-design?
▼ April 2000 – Distill site into one structure – How to re-design redux?
▼ May 2000 – Create production site for real-time user testing – How it is used?
▼ June 2000 – Implement new site and structure – How to reach maintainability?

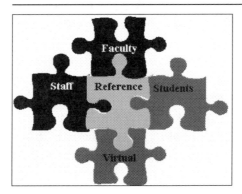

Note: a virtual visitor can be any, all or none of the other four groups.

figure 1. Chart showing target research groups for our libraries' Web site.

Study Methodology – "Users had to be involved!"

As this was the advisory group's first attempt at user-centered design, we did not want to rule out any valid testing methodology; however, our six-month deadline created an urgency that ruled out some forms of testing. The one rule that became our underlying mantra was that our users had to be involved (Karat, 1998). This led us to the three means by which we achieved our outcome. These included:

▼ Focus Groups
▼ Iterative Surveys
▼ Cognitive Interviews

Our focus groups were part of an ongoing initiative at our library to gain user input. The groups were held in our library conference room and provided a free meal to all participants. The moderator of the focus groups took detailed notes and served as an impartial third-party during the focus group process.

During the re-design process our advisory group was able to test ideas among 4 of our known user groups within the settings of the focus groups. These included faculty, staff, graduate and undergraduate students. The advisory group presented different prototypes of our new Web site and asked for input. All of the participants had great ideas; however, some of the focus groups were too controlled by a vocal minority to gain much insight. This was especially evident with users that were already familiar with our site. We found that in most instances expert users of our site did not want change.

The iterative surveys that we analyzed were sequenced attempts (each survey built on several concepts in order to narrow the scope of the concept toward a universal function or definition) at collating user input in regards to terminology that appeared on our site. The surveys focused mainly on vocabulary, both in terms of individual definitions and in terms of definitions relative to the context of our Web site. However, some of these surveys did contain assigned tasks that we asked participants to either explain in narrative or to demonstrate using a computer.

Of these three, the most effective testing method for the advisory group became cognitive interviews. These interviews allowed the interviewer and the subjects to explore the positive and negative usability issues of our Web site without limiting themselves to predefined scripts or surveys. With interested participants, cognitive interviews can really put the designer into the mind of the user group that he/she is trying to reach. Interviews also allow for participants to take the interviewer to deeper levels of understanding if time and participant initiative are available. However, if other means of user input are not combined with cognitive interviews then outcomes can become one-sided much like single-sided focus group input.

January 2000 – Why to Re-Design?

During our first month we began to evaluate our current site and examine other sites for ideas. The advisory group wanted to answer the question, "Why do we need a re-design?" The advisory group also wanted to know how the design could be best suited for our users' needs. To accomplish this task, we asked both librarians and users what they liked best and least about our current site. This was accomplished by interviewing these user groups in the library setting. No script or survey was used; however, each interviewer had a notepad with which to take down comments about the site. Most participants stated that our Web site had never crossed their mind or they liked it because they already knew how to navigate it. Next, the advisory group explored the literature

table 1. Strengths and Weaknesses of Our Old E-Presence

to find out about which testing methods could be used in building the best user-centered site for our libraries. (Appendix A shows the look of our homepage in October 1999 before our re-design)

The following (table 1) are some strengths and weaknesses that we took from our old site via the user and librarian input.

The following (table 2) are 10 of the advisory group's favorite sites that we evaluated and found useful for discovering new ideas about site structure in libraries.

February 2000 – What to Re-Design?

During the second month we also set up an analog survey that was conducted away from the computer to find out which direction should be taken in regards to terminology. We enticed users in the library, Haley Center (the large multi-discipline classroom and office area on campus that also houses the campus bookstore), and in selected English composition classes to take the survey by offering discount coupons redeemable at the Starbuck's coffee shop located in our library. For immediate gratification, we also offered candy. Since the respondents filled out the survey while members of the advisory group were waiting[1] we were able to obtain 100 plus responses within an hour and this was in addition to the responses that we received from the English composition classes. (See Appendix B for survey #1.)

The questions of the survey were specifically designed around information that we had garnered from analyzing our Web site logs. The logs told us that the 5 most used links from our site were:

▼ AUBIECat – our online catalog

▼ Indexes and Databases – our listing of electronic indexes and databases

---

Strengths

▼ Easy for the experienced user to navigate.

▼ Geared towards expert users that wanted to know every service available.

▼ Lots of explanation of the terminology on the page (every link generated a mouse over which explained more about the link).

Weaknesses

▼ New users felt overwhelmed with options.

▼ The download time was too long when using a modem (each mouse over link was a graphic).

▼ The text was too small.

▼ The name AUBIEPlus was too similar to other names being used in the library (Ex. AUBIECat, AUBIExpress)

▼ The dropdown boxes were confusing for users who were new to the Web.

table 1. Strengths and Weaknesses of Our Old E-Presence

---

table 2. Web Advisory
Group's Favorite Library
Web Sites circa. Nov. 1999

▼ Subject Research Guides – our reference guides for finding information in particular subject areas (ex. Aerospace Engineering, English).

▼ Search the Internet – our listing of Web search engines including information on how to search more effectively

▼ Online Reference – a listing of electronic web-based reference materials

From this analysis the group decided to characterize these 5 links as the 5 principle elements of the Auburn University Libraries E-Presence. We also learned that the name of our catalog, AUBIECat, had been well advertised and would definitely be a keeper for the new site. In question 4 in Appendix B (How would you expect to find an item in a journal, magazine, or newspaper on a topic of interest to you?), people most often answered AUBIECat. Did this mean that the general user thought that they could find everything in AUBIECat? Furthermore, most users did not know how to find periodical content on our site.

This formed the foundation for the creation of our prototypes that were designed to test different Web architectures.

Prototype A (figure 2) was developed around a tutorial model where all functions were more fully explained by questions which appeared in the drop-down menu and expert users could follow the *Quick Links* and *All Library Resources* links to get to the sections of the site that they were familiar with.

Prototype B (figure 3) was developed to work with any size screen and was created around the 5 elements of our e-presence that were garnered from the Web logs as described above. The links at the top of the page were used to develop more of a defined e-presence for our architecture and veterinary medical libraries.

Prototype C (figure 4) was developed around our 5 elements and much like Prototype A wanted to define the left hand margin for Quick Links such as **E-Reserves** and **Renew A Book.** The main links on this page also offered mouse-over text that further explained the 5 main element links.

1. MIT	http://libraries.mit.edu/
2. U. of Illinois - Chicago	http://www.uic.edu/depts/lib/
3. Michigan State U.	http://www.lib.msu.edu/
4.Tufts U.	http://www.library.tufts.edu/
5. University of Wisconsin	http://www.library.wisc.edu/
6. Western Michigan U.	http://www.wmich.edu/library/
7. U of Arizona	http://dizzy.library.arizona.edu/
8. Claremont Colleges	http://voxlibris.claremont.edu/
8. UC-Riverside	http://library.ucr.edu/
10. U. of Wisconsin - Lacrosse	http://perth.uwlax.edu/murphylibrary/

table 2. Web Advisory Group's Favorite Library Web Sites circa. Nov. 1999

figure 2. Prototype A

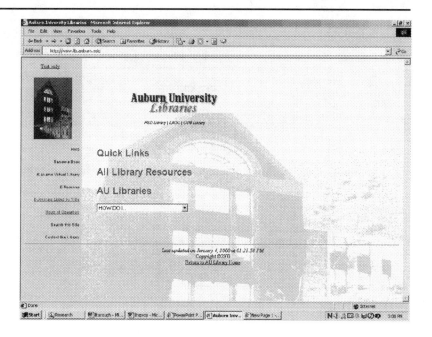

figure 2. Prototype A

Prototype D (figure 5) was created with the 5 elements in mind and offered the same basic layout as Prototype C; however, the main links were all represented with Web text instead of images and the tutorials section was added within the middle column. The Web text change was important as we learned from most of our undergraduate students, a majority of who live off-campus, that they were often times hindered by long download times over their computer modems.

These prototypes were blown up and mounted on poster board and were used with Survey #2 to find out users' initial thoughts concerning the prototypes. (See Appendix C for survey #2.) These tests were again conducted both in the library and in the humanities academic building (Haley Center) utilizing the free giveaways from Starbucks as well as candy. We obtained 100 plus responses.

Survey #2 also showed that users were familiar with the name of our catalog (AUBIECat) and found that some were familiar with the name of our Expanded Academic ASAP full-text database for finding journal articles. Users also understood what the term *reserves* meant. Two schools of thought emerged from this survey from the user standpoint. The first group falls under the category of the "I just want a list!" group and the second being the "Why can't it look like a cool commercial site?" group.

March 2000 – How to Re-Design?

At this point we folded the 4 prototypes into 2 prototypes (Prototypes E and F). We did this by taking the most successful features of our prototypes and the most useful

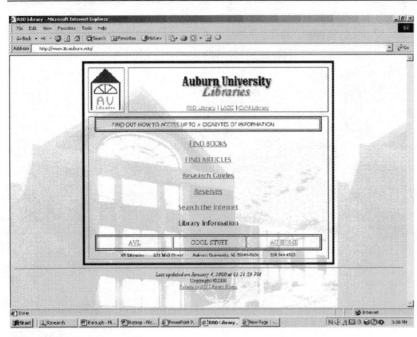

figure 3. Prototype B

figure 3. Prototype B

terminology from our iterative surveys and building them into 2 completely different homepages each utilizing a similar underlying architecture. This was accomplished by dividing the Web Advisory Group into two teams. Each team was to work on a different page. These 2 prototypes were then tested using a cognitive interview script. (See Appendix D.) The script was tested on volunteer student, faculty, and staff members that were interviewed while using our libraries' networked resource computers.

Prototype E (figure 6) stayed much like its predecessor Prototype D but added a scrolling message in the middle column above the Find Books link. Users indicated that such a message was very helpful when found in Prototype F and in comparisons between Prototypes E and F. This Prototype E was chosen over Prototype C because it did not contain the text link images that created longer download times.

Prototype F (figure 7) was found to be lacking in style by most users and when compared with Prototype E seemed too plain for most of the users tested. They felt that more graphics would help. Users did like the scrolling message as well as the simplicity.

From this cognitive interview (See Appendix D) we discovered that the word *reference* could be used from a user standpoint to mean a reference book such as a dictionary or encyclopedia. We also decided to use the term *Find Articles* for the section of our Web site that concerned itself with locating periodical article content. However, this test made us realize that Prototype F did not contain enough access points. Before going any further the committee redesigned Prototype F and added more color and graphics that users had indicated were lacking.

figure 4. Prototype C

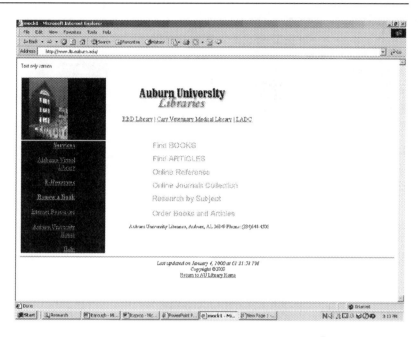

figure 4. Prototype C

Prototype F.1 (figure 8) incorporates the 5 initial element links that we found necessary to include while moving the Quick Links to the lists of services to the right-hand side. This provides users the links that they are likely looking for in the middle of the page where they will not have to search for them. Having our 5 main link elements in the center of the page assures that users will find what they are looking for from our site. Nielsen states, "Web pages should be dominated by content of interest to the user" (Nielsen, Designing Web Usability, 18). By having our ancillary or secondary Quick Links in the right-hand side of the page, users are ready to click, from a GUI standpoint, as the mouse cursor typically hovers toward the right side of the Web page. With the redesigned Prototype F.1 we repeated the previous interview script using Prototypes E and F.1 (See Appendix D) and determined that Prototype F.1 would become the homepage by which we could evolve our libraries' e-presence and Web structure. Our continual redesign with user input had created a winner for everyone.

April 2000 – How to Re-Design Redux?

During the fourth month we began to determine the lower layers of the new Web site and to test their functions and their names. At the same time we began to have open sessions for library faculty and staff to voice concerns about the new site and where it was headed. This was also the time during which we performed what the advisory group

figure 5. Prototype D

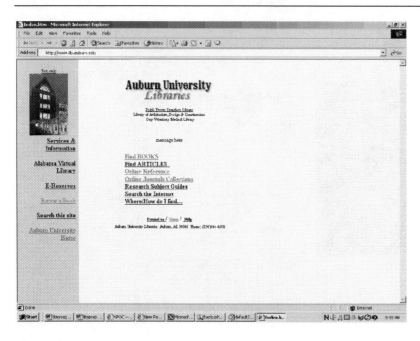

figure 5. Prototype D

liked to call *kamikaze testing* (Nielsen, *Alertbox* 2000). As we tweaked and refined Prototype F.1 we would always interview 3-5 users to see if we needed to create a new cognitive interview script by which to measure our final changes. This proved very effective and was much less time consuming than analyzing 100 surveys or working with interview scripts. However, this was done after we were satisfied that our final product matched our users needs. The volunteers were all rewarded with Starbucks' coupons and were often willing to give 30-45 minutes of their time. This type of kamikaze testing occurred at least twice a week during month four.

Our next interview script, which arose out of our kamikaze testing, focused on specific terminology namely the terms *index* and *Research by Subject*. These terms had plagued us through our entire project and we wanted to at least to try to find user-centered terminology that could represent these concepts. (See Appendix E.)

This interview garnered some great discoveries, namely that users came to our Web site for help with all university Internet technology. (See question 6 Appendix E.) Because of this we greatly expanded the help section on our site to include links to both the university IT Help Desk as well as to information concerning the university computer labs. However, the information that we so desperately needed concerning the terms *index* and *Research by Subject* were still eluding us.

Users clearly did not understand the library meaning of the term *index*. From a user standpoint, the term *index* could be used to mean the index of a book volume but was not clearly understood when used to indicate a source that indexes journal and period-

figure 6. Prototype E

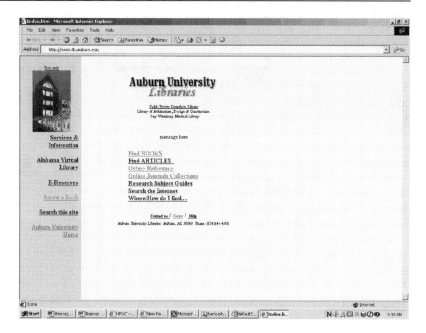

figure 6. Prototype E

ical content. One user stated, "…that word just sounds too British," when referring to the term *index*.

In regards to the term *Research by Subject*, our users were never satisfied with what they found under this link. (See Appendix F.) Most users seemed to expect a type of web portal that searched for only items about particular subjects. For example, say the user was looking for information on *abortion*, they wanted to find a search engine that only gave them information on abortion. This term eventually morphed into the term *Research Guide* but has still proven to be the least effective terminology on our site.

May 2000 – How it is used?

The goal of our fifth month was to get some real-time feedback before our new site went live in June of 2000. What did this mean? It meant that the site had to be ready to go at least one month before its launch in order to both test the new site and to advertise its arrival. This meant that our group was once again split into two teams. One team was working with the technical aspects of the site in order to ascertain its completion while another team changed gears and began to advertise our new e-presence.

Our advertising campaign, as in the business realm, was part "bricks & mortar" and part "bits & bytes." The technical working group implemented the site and advertised its arrival via our old homepage. They also set up a feedback form so that we could get input from our virtual users. (See Appendix G.) The advertising group set up demon-

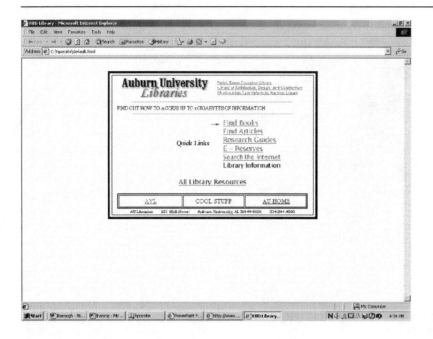

figure 7. Prototype F

figure 7. Prototype F

stration sessions within the confines of our "bricks &mortar" facility for library faculty and staff in order to instruct our personnel in how to use and teach our new site. In addition to this, we incorporated the demonstration sessions into our Faculty/Graduate Student Seminars in order to let faculty know what would be changing in regards to our e-presence.

These sessions were very helpful and proved to be valuable in proof reading the new site for spelling errors and other fine-tuning. The group also realized that even though we had purposefully gathered input from all of our users, that faculty were still not represented as well as they should be. We used the Faculty/Graduate Student Seminar sessions to find out what faculty and other full-time researchers wanted from us. This led to the creation of our Faculty/Graduate Student Services link. This page has proven successful in meeting our faculty needs while still keeping our homepage usable enough for our beginning to intermediate researchers.

June 2000 – Implementation and Maintainability

June came and we implemented our site with very few technical glitches. This was due in large part to the dedication of our advisory group and to the many Auburn users involved with our focus groups, iterative surveys, and cognitive interviews. The site is still a work in progress and we have included our user testing in other aspects of our e-

figure 8. Prototype F.1

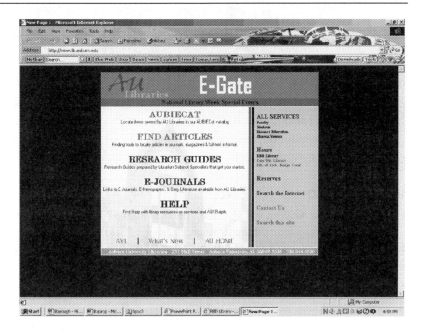

figure 8. Prototype F.1

presence, including the re-design of our online catalog AUBIECat. (See Appendix I and the user suggested idea of a catalog search from our homepage.)

The question that now arises is the maintainability of our user-centric Web. The user is constantly changing in our academic environment. Every year brings a new batch of freshmen, faculty, and staff with multivariate personalities. This will affect our e-presence and will require us to communicate once again with our users and verify whether our current Web scheme is still effective. In many respects, any site that is thinking of planning for and creating maintainability for its usability must be continually refining their usability testing methods and retesting new users on a quarterly and yearly basis.

Conclusions

It is undeniable that the World Wide Web is no longer static. The arrival of dynamic Web sites generated from database content and interactive with the user via the typical Web browser has made static HTML coding obsolete (Antelman, 1). The end result of our re-design project created a main homepage that is beneficial to the inexperienced user while targeting certain user classes such as faculty and graduate students, distance education students, and alumni and visitors. (See Appendix I.) These target groups all need different starting content in order to optimally use our Web site. This has led our Library Technology Department to investigate the customization that can be afforded users through our MYLibrary@Auburn University <mylibrary.auburn.edu> project.

At this time our advisory group is looking for ways to create a completely dynamic e-presence that will not require any static HTML editing. This will allow for optimal content currency. However, our usability work has not been wasted. It has merely caught us up to speed with the rest of the world and with our users. Our project, in fact, has created a new thought process within our organization that seeks to put the user first and then find ways to incorporate those user needs into our organizational goals. The position of Web Development Librarian has also been created during the course of our work and this position and its resources exist to find new initiatives with which to serve our users' needs through technology.

WORKS CITED

Antelman, Kristin. "Getting out of the HTML Business: The Database Driven Web Site Solution." *Information Technology and Libraries* 18(4) (1999): 1.

Karat, Claire-Marie. "Guaranteeing Rights for the User." *Communications of the ACM*, 41(12) (1998): 29-31.

Nielsen, Jakob. "Test with 5 Users." *AlertBox.* (March 19, 2000), http://www.useit.com/altertbox/20000319.html

Nielsen, Jakob. *Designing Web Usability*. Indianapolis: New Riders Publishing, 2000, 18.

The AU Libraries E-Gateway: http://www.lib.auburn.edu

More information about this project can be found at http://www.lib.auburn.edu/wag and at http://www.auburn.edu/~mcdonrh

FOOTNOTES

1. This idea was obtained from watching how students interact with credit card vendors who often stage this same kind of instant gratification giveaway.

APPENDIX A.

AU Libraries Homepage October 1999 – Where we started!

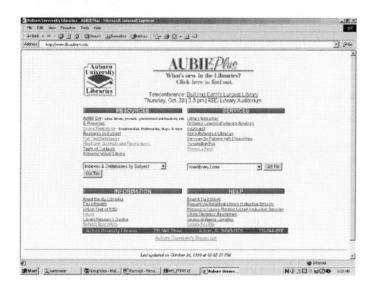

APPENDIX B.

Iterative Survey #1 – Focus on Terminology

In hopes of making the library more user friendly both inside and outside of the library please answer the following questions. Try to answer with the *first words* that come in to your mind and if you can't think of anything then leave the question blank.

What is your current status - (circle one) Fresh., Soph., Jr., Sr., Grad., Faculty, Staff?

If in the course of your research you needed material from a source other than a book what would you use? _____.

What does the term Electronic Journal mean to you? _____.

How would you expect to find an item in a journal, magazine, or newspaper on a topic of interest to you? _____.

How would you describe the item that you found in question #4? _____.

What would you expect to find in a Library Catalog such as AubieCat? _____.

Do you use the library's web page and if so do you use it - (circle one) a lot, some, a little, none at all?

The library's web page would be easier to use if?

_____
_____
_____.

If you would like to be contacted for further input please fill out the following:

Name_____
Address_____
Email_____Phone_____

APPENDIX C.
Iterative Survey #2 – Focus on Terminology
HOMEPAGE REVIEW FORM

Favorite: A   B   C   D   E

Current Status: Fresh. Soph. Jr.   Sr.   Grad. Faculty   Staff

If you saw a book on Amazon.com, and you wanted to check to see if the AU Library had a copy, where would you click?

If your teacher said you had to find 3 journal or magazine articles on a particular subject, and none were available free on the Internet, where would you click?

If your instructor put the course syllabus and notes on the library's electronic reserve and you needed to view or print them, where would you click?

Do you have any other comments on what you like or don't like about this page?

APPENDIX D.
Cognitive Interview Script #1

Current Status: Fresh. Soph. Jr.   Sr.   Grad. Faculty   Staff

1. USING THE FIRST MOCKUP PAGE
If your teacher said you had to find 3 journal or magazine articles on a particular

subject, and none were available for free in the Internet, where would you click?

You need to use an encyclopedia or dictionary and the library is closed, so you'd like to find any that the library has access to electronically. Where would you click?

2. USING THE SECOND MOCKUP PAGE
If your teacher said you had to find 3 journal or magazine articles on a particular subject, and none were available for free in the Internet, where would you click?

You need to use an encyclopedia or dictionary and the library is closed, so you'd like to find any that the library has access to electronically. Where would you click?

WHICH PAGE DO YOU LIKE BETTER?   1   2
WHY?

WHAT OTHER GENERAL COMMENTS DO YOU HAVE?

APPENDIX E.
Cognitive Interview Script #2

Circle Floor of Library
1   2   3   4

1. What is your current status: Fr   So   Jr   Sr   Fac   Staff   Visitor

2. What information can you get from "AubieCat"?
(PLEASE CIRCLE ALL THAT APPLY.)
    Email Directory of all library employees
    A directory of phone numbers of all library employees
    One email address to send questions/comments
    The main contact address and phone number for the library
    All of the above
    Other:

5. If you clicked on a link from the library's home page that said "Research by Subject" what would you expect to see?

6. From the library's home page, if you clicked on a "Help" link, what options would you expect to see? (PLEASE CIRCLE ALL THAT APPLY.)
    Information describing how to do research
    Technological assistance on how to connect to databases from home

A question "hot line" (phone number) that you could call and talk to a librarian
An email address to send questions/comments
All of the above
Other:

7. What other general comments/observations do you have concerning the libraries' home page?

APPENDIX F.

What users found under our Research by Subject Link.

A

- Accountancy
- Aerospace Engineering
- Agriculture Economics and Rural Sociology
- Agronomy and Soils
- Animal and Dairy Sciences
- Anthropology
- Architecture
- Art
- Aviation Management

B

- Biological Sciences
- Biomedical Sciences
- Biosystems Engineering
- Business

APPENDIX G.
Online Survey during testing of our new site.

SURVEY SAYS!

AU Libraries e-gateway

Home | AubieCat | All Services | Search Site | Help

Thank you for expressing your willingness to help! We appreciate your assistance in testing the new Web site for the AU Libraries. Your suggestions and comments will be given full consideration.

Do you like the look of our new Web site?
- ⦿ Yes
- ○ No
- ○ Not Sure

Do you like the way our new Web site is organized?
- ⦿ Yes
- ○ No
- ○ Not Sure

What do you like best about our Web site?

What about our Web site could be improved?

Name:

E-Mail:

- ⦿ AU Undergraduate Student
- ○ AU Graduate Student
- ○ AU Faculty
- ○ AU Staff
- ○ AU Alumni
- ○ Non-AU

How are you accessing our Web site:

- ⦿ Campus
- ○ Off-Campus

[Send Comments]   [Clear Comments Form]

47

APPENDIX H.

Our Faculty Graduate Student Services Page

Notice that the java script expandable menus at the top give long lists of options for experienced users.

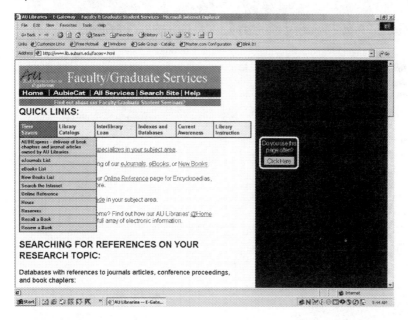

APPENDIX I.

Our Current Web Site – Where We Are Now!

chapter 5

Structured Observation and Protocol Analysis
Using Video Split-Screen Technology for Evaluating Web Site Usability
William J. Gibbs

Background

In the mid 1990s Eastern Illinois University's Booth Library, like many university libraries, began to incorporate the Web into its services. Media Services, a department within the Library, initially used this evolving medium as an information dissemination and retrieval tool and then gradually employed it for instructional purposes. With the exponential growth of the Web and increasing reliance on it, personnel in Media Services expressed a need to evaluate and potentially refine the department's Web site.

This paper presents a discussion of Media Services' use of the Web and the vital role the medium plays in providing services to the University community. The paper also discusses methods used to evaluate the Web site and the results from the evaluation.

Description of the University and Department

Established in 1895, Eastern Illinois University is a midwestern university with approximately 10,500 students. It is principally an undergraduate institution with a tradition in teacher preparation. It has comprehensive undergraduate programs in the arts, sciences, humanities, and professions. The Graduate School provides programs at the master's and specialist's levels.

49

Central to the University is Booth Library, and housed within the Library is the department of Media Services. A principal function of Media Services is to assist with the infusion of learning technologies into educational processes. It is concerned primarily with applications of technology to teaching and learning and is comprised of three units: educational technology services, technology system services (hardware distribution and maintenance), and production services (graphic design and photography). While many of the services provided are highly technical, they are directed at how to best utilize technology to enhance pedagogical processes and student learning. To this end, personnel provide experiences, support, programs, and products that improve faculty technical knowledge and skills and assist them with integrating technology into the curriculum.

Media Services plays a central role in the University's academic technology efforts in four areas: 1) instructional technology training; 2) instructional technology project design and development; 3) faculty development facilities and consulting areas, and 4) instructional technology deployment and maintenance.

The System Studied

The system chosen for evaluation was the Media Services' Web site. It is a comprehensive site employing a variety of media (video, audio, text, etc.) for information delivery. Given the nature of the site, department personnel felt that ongoing assessments were needed to critique and refine it.

Prior to 1997, the Web site was used primarily for information delivery purposes. Users could, for example, obtain information about services, prices, hours, and personnel. However, in 1997, Media Services developed a technology-training initiative, which greatly influenced the design of the site. The initiative had the following objectives:

▼ To improve the faculty's ability to effectively and appropriately utilize and integrate computer technology into the teaching and learning process.

▼ To provide support to faculty as they begin to integrate computer technology into their teaching.

▼ To provide learning experiences and products to foster a willingness on the part of the faculty to make an investment in using technology for teaching and learning.

▼ To provide learning experiences and products that foster easy and immediate success with using technology for teaching and learning.

From the initiative grew a greater reliance on the Web for disseminating and collecting information as well as providing instruction and instructional support to classes. The initiative proposed eight types of Web resources (Gibbs, 2000), each of which is described below:

▼ Instruction: On-line tutorials and instructional lessons were to be delivered on the Web providing users access to this content twenty-four hours a day.

▼ Profiles: Expert profiles that featured case summaries, examples, reviews, and results of faculty who integrated technology into the teaching and learning process were to be compiled and disseminated on the Web.

▼ Electronic Lesson Plans (ELP): ELP were designed to make it easy for faculty to use Web materials in their teaching. The ELP were discipline-specific lesson plans accompanied by strategies for using Web-based materials, student Web pages, and worksheets, etc. The ELP were dynamic documents allowing additions, modifications, and updates to be done on-line.

▼ Virtual Instructional Support and Help Desk: An electronic discussion forum created to answer questions about topics covered under any area of Media Services' training initiative.

▼ On-Line Projects: Noteworthy projects developed on-campus or nationally were sought and then previewed through the Web site to provide incentive to faculty for effectively using technology.

▼ Web Site for Research on Learning Technologies: The Web Site for Research on Learning Technologies provided faculty research literature related to the educational technology field.

▼ Web Site for Product Information: This site provided faculty a means to locate a database of information on third-party software and hardware products that would be useful to them for teaching and learning.

▼ Software Resources: This site previewed software applications, including trial and beta versions and freeware. These applications were located in a central location on the Web to allow faculty easy access to them.

Reasons for Undertaking Study

There were three reasons for the study. First, as the medium evolved and demand for Web services grew resulting from the initiative, the amount of information and materials at the site increased dramatically. Because of the variety of individuals adding to the site over the years, materials often lacked uniformity and visual and programmatic appeal. Second, a significant portion of the site included instructional tutorials on various topics, such as software. As an orientation, the department required new employees to study the tutorials and become proficient at using them to learn new software programs. As these individuals used the tutorials, "gaps" were identified in the instructions and site design. For instance, one new staff member commented that the tutorials assumed a level of proficiency beyond what he possessed and thus he could not efficiently use them as a learning tool. Third, software evaluation was an integral process in departmental operations. Media Services' personnel routinely evaluated instructional software programs delivered on CD-ROM and other disk media but no formal ongoing evaluation had been undertaken of the Web site.

Methods

Media Services used multiple data collection methods to assess the usability of the site, including structured observation and protocol analysis using video-split-screen technology (Gibbs & Shapiro, 1994), computer usage logs, and surveys. For this paper, only the structured observation and protocol analysis method with video-spilt-screen is discussed.

Video-split-screen Technology

When using a video-split-screen method for usability testing, users are video recorded as they interact with a software program. For the evaluation discussed here, four subjects, three females and one male, each participated in a single evaluation session, which lasted approximately two hours. Subjects were undergraduate and graduate student employees of Media Services. While they had knowledge of the department, they possessed little or no prior experience with the department's Web site. On average, subjects indicated that they had used computers for six years; they used computers for four hours per week; and they completed three computer courses. Subjects rated their computer proficiency as five (moderate) on a ten-point scale.

The researchers used a structured observation and protocol analysis approach to record observations of subjects using the Web site. They asked subjects to explore Media Services' Web site and to think aloud. The researchers gave the following directions:

> "Try to think aloud. I guess you often do so when you are alone and working on a problem. The main thing is to talk aloud constantly from the minute you see the computer screen. We want to get everything you happen to think of, no matter how irrelevant it may seem."

Subjects critiqued the site, suggested revisions, discussed misunderstandings or provided any commentary that would contribute to improving it. They could spend as much time or as little time as they wanted on the task. Periodically, the researchers prompted them to speak up or tell what they were thinking.

A video effects generator combined two images (subject and computer screen) so the researchers, when viewing the videotape, could observe the computer screen, including mouse movements, object (e.g., buttons, links, etc.) selections, and page changes simultaneously with the subject's behavior and vocal expressions. When the researchers reviewed videotapes, the subject appeared on the left portion of the monitor and the computer screen image appeared on the right. They subsequently transcribed verbal commentaries from the videotapes. The technique provided observations of users' actions and decisions, verbal commentary and elaboration, and non-verbal and attitudinal reactions. It also provided a permanent visual and auditory account of observation sessions for subsequent analysis.

Ericsson and Simon (1984) suggested that verbalizations made during an instructional activity (e.g., studying a tutorial) reveal an individual's thoughts in short-term-memory. This was particularly interesting to the researchers since tutorials and instructionally oriented lessons comprised a substantial portion of the Web site. Analysis of users' information processes when performing Web-based activities could provide greater understanding of how such activities impact learning. With structured observations and protocol analysis, it is possible to identify the type and level (e.g., superficial, higher-level) of information processing in which users engage as well as their focus of attention. For example, by analyzing verbalizations, one can determine whether users are processing the instructional content of a Web-based tutorial superficially, deeply, or not at all. Moreover, the characteristics (e.g., design, media, language, accessibility, etc.) of the tutorial can be observed to assess their impact on processing levels.

The researchers reviewed all commentary and indicated (Yes or No) whether or not a comment was valuable to the purpose of the study. They segmented each comment based on its meaning and coded the information contained in the comment segment (Ericsson & Simon, 1993). Table 1 is the coding scheme used to code subject commentary. It is a modification of the coding scheme used by Nakhleh and Krajcik (1991, p.11).

Technology Used

The hardware used for the evaluations included a personal computer connected to the Internet and equipped with a Web browser (e.g., Netscape). A Super-VHS video camera and lapel microphone recorded subjects during the evaluations. A scan converter connected to the computer converted the computer's digital output to an analog signal. A video special effects generator mixed the outputs of the camera and scan converter and sent them to a S-VHS recorder. Review of evaluations took place using a standard VHS player and monitor. The researchers parsed and coded commentary using a word processor and a spreadsheet. Two researchers conducted the evaluations.

Time Devoted to Evaluations

Assessing a hypermedia informational and instructional system such as the Web site described in this paper can be time consuming. In fact, Nemetz, et al. 1997 caution about usability testing with potential users due to, among other things, the increased time associated with evaluation. Their paper discusses heuristic evaluation as a less costly (in time) alternative using a small number of expert evaluators rather than potential users. In this study, subjects spent, on average, two hours in evaluation. Subsequent to the evaluations, the researchers spent numerous hours transcribing notes and videotape dialogue, reviewing the videotapes, and coding commentary.

What Was Learned?
Analysis of Commentary

Working independently, three reviewers coded subjects' commentary. They coded the majority of commentary as *Analytical* (33.23%), *Procedural* (21.14%), *Hesitation* (11.82%), and *Commentary* (16.79%) (See Table 2).

table 1. Coding Categories

CODING CATEGORIES:

I. Procedural statements refer to actions (mental or physical) that the user performs in the software. (P1-P6)

    1.   Reading/examining information (text, graphics, video, audio).

    2.   Examining events occurring in the software (e.g., response time, visual-animated displays, hyper linking ("I clicked and it took me to this page?" error messages).

    3.   Questioning (e.g., information, action).

    4.   Stating a goal (the intent to perform an action).

    5.   Deciding what to do next (Deliberating as to what action to perform).

    6.   Statement to indicate that the user is performing an action.

II. Analytical statements referring to (A1-A7):

    1.   Explaining information or events.

    2.   The user explains his/her own actions.

    3.   Recalling pertinent subject matter knowledge (about the content, or the browser or browser functionality).

    4.   Making observations—this is different than P1 (examining information) in that the user is examining information or events and based on this examination makes observations.

    5.   Demonstrating understanding of specific information or events.

    6.   Demonstrating misunderstanding of specific observations related to the information or events.

    7.   Hypothesizing/speculating about concepts, information, or events.

III. Statements expressing inadequate understanding of information or events related to the browser. (S1)

IV. Statements expressing adequate understanding of information or events related to the browser. (S2)

V. Confusion (F) (Statements expressing confusion—these are statements in which a culmination of information or events has perplexed the user. The user may be unaware of why they are confused. These statements are not tied to any specific observation, information, or event.)

VI. Emotional statements referring to:

    1.   Statements exhibiting frustration (E1)

    2.   Statements exhibiting satisfaction (E2)

VII. Exclamatory (Ex1) (Indicates the emotion, which is not the result of puzzlement, frustration or satisfaction. The exclamatory expression is of no communication value—the reaction does not relate to the content or information.)

VIII. Hesitation (H) (Used as fillers while the subject is thinking, such as hum, Ah.)

IX. Commentary (C) (The remarks made about patterns or pages, which are not related to the information for which the subject is searching. These remarks are made without emotional reactions.)

table 1. Coding Categories *(Modified from Nakhleh & Krajcik, 1991, pp.11)*

table 2. Percentage of
Comments by Coding
Category

Reviewers coded 16.79% of comments as *Commentary*, which were remarks about Web pages unrelated to the review task or information for which the subject was searching. These remarks were made without emotional reactions. For example, the following statements were coded as *Commentary*: *"...I have some computer understanding, I know all about WordPerfect..."* , *"I thought this was something totally different maybe it's just ignorant [sic] on my part because I didn't like to read them. ",* *"I mean, like Macintosh's scare me..."*

The second type of most coded comment was *Hesitation* (11.82%) or "fillers", such as "Um" or "Ah". *Analytical* statements indicative of subjects making observations constituted 11.61% of the coded commentary. In response to the amount of time and steps needed to access specific informational sections of the Web site, a respondent stated, *"...it takes kind of long to get there."* Accordingly, responding to the positioning of buttons, a respondent stated, *"...see I think these should be on top."* Several subjects making similar observational type comments can be useful for identifying problems that other users may encounter.

Reviewers coded 10.16% of the commentary as *Procedural* statements, specifically those indicative of reading/examining information (text, graphics, video, audio). They coded the following statements as procedural, *"...click below to see, uh...."*, *"...Instructional Systems Services"*, *"...Instructional Design"*, *"...Production Services."* Even though these comments are comprised of only a few words, they do indicate that subjects read the information. It is interesting to note that upon review of the videotapes, subjects appeared to approach the analysis of the Web site methodically and not haphazardly. They read the text information and, based on it, decided how and where to proceed.

The reviewers coded ninety-nine statements (4.01%) as *Confusion*, which indicated that a culmination of information or events perplexed the user. This is important information. While the percentage is low in comparison to other categories, it represents a

Percentages (%)

P1	P2	P3	P4	P5	P6
10.16	2.79	2.71	0.73	2.59	3.16
A1	A2	A3	A4	A5	A6
7.97	7.65	1.90	11.61	2.71	1.38
S1	S2	F	E1	E2	Ex1
3.28	2.14	4.01	1.25	4.13	1.21
H	C				
11.82	16.79				

table 2. Percentage of Comments by Coding Category
(See Table 1 for code listing)

55

problem in that aspects of the site may confuse some users. The following dialogue illustrates one subject's confusion:

"Too many words. I don't know if it's supposed to be there because there are so many, I don't know, it's like here pick one and then it's like this all of the sudden...Oh, no."

Accordingly, the reviewers coded 31 statements (1.25%) as *Emotional* or statements exhibiting frustration. Statements such as, "...that doesn't make any sense." or "Where was I, Systems Services..." indicate that the user is becoming frustrated. Subjects' nonverbal responses and tonal fluctuations in verbal responses reinforce this observation and seemingly reflected the users' growing frustration.

The commentary analysis afforded the researchers an opportunity to observe, in a general way, users' thinking as they studied the Web site. A general review of the commentary suggests that subjects primarily engaged in *Analytical* (33.23%) and *Procedural* (21.14%) type activities when reviewing the site. It is useful to see that while there were statements indicative of user confusion and frustration, the number of these types of comments was low, relatively speaking. High percentages of comments in these categories would seemingly necessitate major site and content revisions. Nevertheless, the observation that subjects engaged in *Analytical* and *Procedural* type activities may be a reflection of the inquiry task. The researchers asked subjects to review a Web site and to think aloud when doing so and this may have influenced them to make statements of the *Analytical* and *Procedural* type. Users without these instructions may not have made critical reviews of the Web site and so a more diverse commentary coding could have resulted.

Text Information

Subject reviews of the Web site helped identify two fundamental issues regarding information presented in text form. First, in this study, subjects attended to text information and it appeared to influence how they proceeded to use the site.

At various stages of development over the years since 1997, developers converted print documents such as departmental information brochures into HTML pages. In some cases, the developers gave little thought to text length, writing style, textual information in HTML format, or navigation. As subjects traversed these online documents, the researchers observed that they initially appeared to search for contextual clues on Web pages rather than graphical or pictorial clues. For example, while the Web pages within the site contained graphics and photographs, subjects read or searched through the textual information to seemingly become oriented and make decisions about how to proceed. Certain graphical elements (e.g., buttons) attracted attention, but subjects also reviewed the text and appeared to use it to derive understanding of a page. Thus, their approach to using the site was, to some extent, systematic and purposeful and directed by the text information. This observation may be due, in part, to the nature of the evaluation task and the participating subjects. It is plausible that users unaffiliated with Media Services, unlike the subjects in this study, when arriving at the site, may randomly click buttons and scan the information without attending to details in the text.

Moreover, a subject's motivation is likely to influence the extent to which he attends to text details. When asked about the text of a page, a subject responded with the following:

> "There's a lot. Um, and it looks, it looks kind of crowded, but I guess it depends on my purpose for being in here. If I was just curious about what Media Service was, you know just out of curiosity, I'm not sure I'd go through reading all of this. It depends on what kind of time and if I was doing research or something like that and if it was important, then I guess it's not that big a deal. So, each one of these things now is a way to get around. Ok. Um, same thing here. I guess it would, uh, I don't know, it might be a little clumsy putting blocks everywhere, especially if it's in the middle of the text like right here."

Nonetheless, this observation was not dismissed and provided valuable information to the site developers for the writing of Web page content. Writing style, flow, and directives suggested in the textual information received greater focus than previously given.

Second, subjects indicated that many Web pages contained too much text and were over-crowded. From the study, a concerted effort was made to limit excess verbiage on Web pages.

Colors and Graphic Elements

Subjects in the study recommended color choices, highlighting, and graphic elements for the Web pages. These elements directly impacted how they perceived the site. For example, the following transcript indicates how a subject perceives a line as a separator between departmental units and a recommendation is made to make the line more pronounced to delineate between units.

> "…the SMC here is from this real thin line down to I guess this same type of line here. Um, actually, this line, the purple line, looks more appropriate as a divider between departments. Um, the divider between departments I think should be more pronounced than this purple line."

What is significant about this transcript is the perceived meaning the subject assigns to the "thin line", a separator between departmental units. Such observations caused the developers to be more purposeful in their use of graphic elements.

Conclusions

The video-split-screen method was effective for assessing the Web site. Media Services has made several revisions to its site based on data collected using the video-split-screen method. Figure 1 is the present home page and represents a revision of the initial site. Figure 2 illustrates an updated and not yet released version of the Web site. The video recordings enabled the researchers to rebuild (visually and aurally) the actions taken by subjects. This was beneficial for several reasons. First, it allowed them to monitor subjects' use of the Web site, the options they selected, and their reactions. It also showed where subjects were confused and what they liked and disliked. Second, the method allowed subjects to respond immediately as problems occurred and to provide feedback about them. Among other things, this helped the researchers determine, to

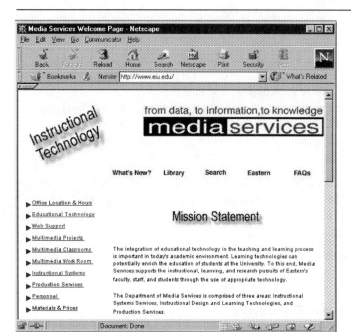

figure 1. Media Services
Home Page

figure 1. Media Services Home Page

some extent, the severity of the problem and its impact on users. Third, the method provided the researchers a means to review and validate the observations of other reviewers (Gibbs & Shapiro, 1994).

Coding subject commentary allowed the researchers to examine the types of comments made about the Web site and, in a general way, observe how the site, its contents, and media influenced users' thinking patterns. The researchers observed that, to a large extent, subjects engaged in analytical and procedural type activity, which helped focus site redesign efforts on related issues. For example, reviewers coded approximately 3% of the commentary as *Procedural, deciding what to do next. (Deliberating as to what action to perform).* Statements in this category reflect the users' deliberation about how to go on in the site. The subject statement, "...*this way to get back, I guess.*" reflects uncertainty about how to proceed and is indicative of design flaws. Categorizing comments and counting code frequencies give the designer a general view of the types of design problems that exist and how they can potentially divert and/or direct user attention. As problem types become evident, designers can employ the video-split-screen method to analyze and reconstruct, in a detailed manner, design flaws encountered by users.

The researchers noted that the hardware necessary to complete the evaluations and the time required for data analysis as the two primary disadvantages of the video-split-screen approach. The method affords researchers a wealth of data to be studied. The amount of data obtained, while beneficial, requires a large investment of time for analysis. The video-split-screen method needs to be compared to other approaches to evaluate the

figure 2. Media Services
Home Page (Revised)

figure 2. Media Services Home Page (Revised)

benefits of the results in relationship to the time and cost involved. It may be that less time-consuming and costly methods yield similar results to the one discussed here.

WORKS CITED

Nakhleh, M. B., & Krajcik, J. S. (1991). The use of videotape to analyze the correspondence between the verbal commentary of students and their actions when using different levels of instrumentation during laboratory activities. Paper presented at the annual meeting of the National Association for Research in Science Teaching, Lake Geneva, WI.

Ericsson, K. A. & Simon, H. A. (1993). *Protocol analysis verbal reports as data.* Cambridge, Massachusetts: The MIT Press.

Ericsson, K., & Simon, H. A. (1984). *Protocol analysis verbal reports as data.* Cambridge, Massachusetts: The MIT Press.

Gibbs, W.J. (2000). Media Services: Technology training initiatives. *Illinois Association for Educational Communications and Technology Journal*, Volume 5, 18-23.

Gibbs, W.J. & Shapiro, A.F. (1994). Video-split-screen technology: A data collection instrument. *Journal of Computing in Higher Education*, 5(2), 113-121.

Nemetz F., Winckler M. A. A., de Lima, J. V. *Evaluating evaluation methods for hypermedia applications.* ED-MEDIA & ED-TELECOM 97. 1997, Calgary - Canada.

The Department of Media Services, Eastern Illinois University Booth Library:
http://www.eiu.edu/~mediasrv

chapter 6

Working with Consultants to Test Usability
The Indiana University Bloomington Experience

Julianne Bobay, Diane Dallis, Gwendolyn Pershing and Mary Pagliero Popp

1. Introduction

In the spring of 1999, Indiana University Bloomington Libraries contracted with two consultants to help review goals for the Libraries' Web site, to lead usability tests with various user groups, and to provide a plan for the architecture of the site.

At that time, the Indiana University Bloomington Libraries (IUB) had developed a very large and rich web site. The site had developed in the libraries over the prior four years in an "organic" manner: a consciously chosen decentralized approach that encouraged individual initiative and participation in web development throughout the libraries. Library units (branch libraries, library departments, etc.,) were given the authority, the tools and a structure in which to develop rich content that best suited the needs of their primary users, and they went at it with vigor.

The resulting web site, encompassing more than 5,000 pages, is actually a loosely knit federation of individual sub-sites, some of which are quite noteworthy and have received national attention. This collection of sub-sites is bound together by a mandated template that all library units must use. The template ensures consistent headers, logos, colors, and page layouts, as well as functionality across browsers, equipment, etc.

Over the years as the site grew larger, navigation became inadequate and the site posed usability problems. The size and decentralized structure of the site also led to problems with maintenance. These and other problems of an "organically-grown" site resulted in the decision by the IUB Libraries to engage outside consultants to conduct usability testing and provide advice on how to evolve the site to its next level.

Following discussions with a usability specialist from the Indiana University Information Technology Services, and interviews with potential consultants, the IUB Libraries contracted with two consulting firms and the IUB usability specialist to lead an evaluation of the IUB Libraries web site. The consulting firms had complementary skills and expertise, and they agreed to work together on the project. One consulting firm, Gomoll Research and Design, recommended to the IUB Libraries by University Information Technology Services, specialized in user-centered design and field research, and had worked primarily with corporate clients. The second consulting firm, Argus Associates, had its roots in the library world, had a staff that included many librarians, and had consulted on web design and information architecture in both library and corporate spheres.

The IUB Libraries web evaluation was conducted in two stages. The usability consulting firm and the IUB usability specialist performed field tests and usability studies. They also interviewed library administrators and web developers. They issued design recommendations based on the data collected. Those findings were used as background information by the information architecture consultants for the in-depth analysis of the site itself and investigations of the suitability and sustainability of various information architectures.

The Libraries appointed a Web Assessment/Architecture Working Group to work with both consultants. This group was composed of librarians and library staff who had been actively involved in developing library web resources, as well as individuals with new perspectives for further development of the site. The formal charge to this group included:

▼ helping consultants to identify audiences/stakeholders
▼ drafting library goals for the web site
▼ providing documents, background information and data to the consultants about the present web site and its development
▼ establishing goals for the web site assessment project
▼ providing input and facilitating the usability research by identifying users/participants
▼ providing input on the plan
▼ assisting with survey administration and with data analysis
▼ facilitating communications within the IUB Libraries

2. Preparing for Consultants

The Web Assessment/Architecture Working Group (Working Group) provided historical context in preparation for the consultants' work. They performed a study of use statistics, identifying the most heavily used parts of the site by internal and external users,

61

and tracked changes in use patterns. In addition, the Web Assessment/Architecture Working Group drafted the following goals to guide the consultants' work. These goals echoed a "vision statement" for the web site prepared in March 1998 by the Libraries' Web Policy Committee, and were approved by the Libraries Management Team in February 1999.

Primary Goal

"The IUB Libraries' public web site will be judged by our primary users, (students, faculty and staff in Bloomington and on other campuses,) as the BEST site to find the scholarly information they need for their teaching, research and studies. The web site is a critical component of the set of services and resources that make up the IUB Libraries, and will provide members of the IUB community with a centralized entry point for information about and access to all library resources in printed and electronic form."

Other Goals

"In addition to serving the research and teaching needs of the faculty, students and staff of Indiana University, the Libraries' web site will provide users from the community, the state, the country and the world with:

▼ accurate information describing and spotlighting the IUB Libraries collections, services and achievements, especially those that have national or international visibility and interest.

▼ well-organized and usable access to internet resources created or selected by subject specialists throughout the IUB Libraries.

The content and organization of the site will capitalize on the abilities and knowledge of staff and librarians throughout the libraries to create, maintain and continually develop web resources and services.

The IUB Libraries' web site will provide a positive impression on all visitors to the site, acknowledging that users' satisfaction is determined by many factors, ranging from the availability and ease of finding of key resources to visual and aesthetic concerns."

3. Stage 1
Usability Tests, Field Studies, and Surveys

During February and March 1999, the usability consultants conducted in-depth user research in order to more thoroughly understand how the IUB Libraries web site was being used, to pinpoint areas for improvement, and to plan for a re-designed web site. Seventeen participants were selected by the Working Group to participate in field studies or usability sessions. These participants represented the widest possible range of user groups and perspectives, and included five faculty, four graduate students, and four undergraduate students from social sciences, sciences, humanities; three mem-

table 1. Usability Test Tasks

bers of university staff; and one outside person. The individuals came with a wide range of experience in both computing and in library research.

Usability Studies: Consultants and working group members observed and video-taped eight study participants in a usability laboratory as they used the Libraries' web site to perform specific typical tasks. The Working Group developed the list of tasks below for the usability studies, many of which were designed to explore known or suspected areas of difficulty.

Field Studies: With the participation of the Working Group and input from the information architecture consultants, the usability consultants planned and conducted field studies with eight participants. During the field visits, consultants and members of the Working Group interviewed, observed and videotaped participants in their natural work environments as they performed tasks they would normally use the web site to accomplish. Observing the current use of the web site allowed the usability consultants to identify ways the site could be improved to better suit users' needs.

Surveys: In order to focus the libraries' attention on the primary use of the web site, the usability consultants administered a survey to identify the "top ten" tasks users did

Usability study tasks:

1. Where would you check to see if the IU Bloomington library has a copy of the book *Catcher in the Rye*?

2. You are researching about the causes of panic attacks. Find a list of references to journal articles on this topic.

3. You plan to stay and get some work done during spring break next week. When will the main library be open?

4. Find information about the Indiana University Digital Library Program. What is it and who is involved in the program?

5. You know that the IUB Libraries have a very good collection of manuscripts of Sylvia Plath. How can you find more information about this collection from the library's web site?

6. You are a student at IUB, and your professor has given you a reference to an article she wants you to read in a journal called *Communications of the ACM*. Find a link to the electronic version of the journal.

7. Your book from the HPER [Health Physical Education and Recreation] library is due today. You want to keep it longer. How can you request this from the library's web site?

8. You are a returning adult student taking one class a semester and rarely visit any library on campus. You need to copy some articles your professor said he put on reserve. Find out if the libraries have the required readings on reserve for your H105 history class with Mr. Katz.

9. Does the IU library at Bloomington have a collection about Poland? Who is the librarian in charge of the Polish collection and how can you contact that person?

10. You are an instructor, and your student asks you how to prepare a bibliographic citation for an article he obtained from an electronic journal. Can you find such information from the library's web site?

11. Imagine that you are a faculty member who is involved in publishing a book. You need to know how ISBN numbers are assigned. How would you use the library's web site to find out who assigns those numbers and additional information about the process?

12. Imagine that your research area is English Literature and you want to find what internet resources are available. What location on the library's web site would lead you to a listing of recommended internet resources on this subject?

table 1. Usability Test Tasks

63

at the library web site. The survey consisted of a list of twenty tasks developed by the Working Group based on web use statistics and their experience. The consultants asked the seventeen participants in field studies and usability studies, as well as library administrators and web developers, to perform two rankings on the list: listing the ten most important and ten most frequent tasks they did at the site.

To supplement the information gathered from the usability consultants' survey, the Working Group made available a web-based version of the survey to all users of the site. In this survey, participants were asked to rank the same list of twenty tasks, but instead of doing two rankings (importance and frequency,) they were asked to rank only by frequency. The Working Group decided to do this after observing the study participants struggle with the often difficult and time-consuming process of two rankings, and decided that it was unlikely that the web survey respondents would be as motivated to

table 2. Users' Top Twenty Tasks

The twenty tasks on the survey were:

- ▼   Locate information describing the IUB Libraries' collections and services
- ▼   Use IUCAT, the IU Libraries online catalog
- ▼   Read an electronic journal online
- ▼   Verify a citation
- ▼   Use a library database for information on a topic (e.g., ERIC, Academic Search Elite)
- ▼   Ask a question
- ▼   Contact a particular librarian or library specialist in my subject field
- ▼   Recommend a book, journal, or database for purchase by a library
- ▼   Request that materials be placed on reserve for a class
- ▼   Guide students in your classes in their research projects
- ▼   Learn about library instruction sessions or request a library instruction session
- ▼   Locate handouts or tutorials about how to use library resources and services
- ▼   Complete a transaction with the library (e.g., renew a book, request an interlibrary loan)
- ▼   Find "when and where" information about the libraries (e.g., hours, locations, workshops)
- ▼   Get help/get started on library research
- ▼   Find materials on reserve for your classes
- ▼   Find public information about the libraries: press releases, announcements, statistics, etc.
- ▼   Search the World Wide Web for information on a research topic
- ▼   Learn about career opportunities
- ▼   Use librarian-created views of the web to find research materials in a discipline

table 2. Users' Top Twenty Tasks

figure 1. User Survey Task Rankings

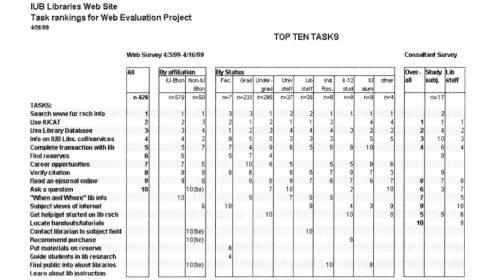

figure 1. User Survey Task Rankings

contribute as much time as the study participants. Each person who participated in the web survey was entered in a drawing for $25 or $100 gift certificates for the university bookstore. To encourage users to complete the survey, a button was added to the IUB Libraries homepage and to many sub-site homepages labeled "Win $100". Demographic data on survey respondents was gathered, but the surveys themselves were guaranteed to be anonymous. Respondents were required to fill out a brief demographic information form that indicated their status, department/school, campus, major, job title, and their frequency of web use before accessing the survey itself. Results were sent to two files on the server. Each respondent's email address was checked against a list of respondents to make sure no user submitted multiple surveys. The username list was kept separate from the survey responses. The responses, including the demographic info, the domain name of the computer where the survey was filled out, and the survey ranking were stored in a delimited flat file which was imported into Excel for analysis and manipulation.

Of 626 responses, 7 were from faculty, 233 were from graduate students, and 295 were from undergraduate students. Results were in general consistent with the top-ten list developed by the consultants; nine of the "top ten" tasks in the two lists are the same. There were, however, important and sometimes subtle differences among various user groups. Because of the population demographics of the web-based survey, functionalities that were relevant to instructors did not make the top-ten list on the web survey (e.g., place materials on reserve,) and functionalities of particular interest to students ranked high (e.g., find information on career opportunities). Only six of the top ten tasks identified in the web survey made the librarians/library staff "10 most important" tasks. In addition, the web survey documented important differences between users affiliated with IU and those coming in from the outside.

These data support the very important caveat that surveying large populations and generalizing the results can mask important differences among user populations. Analyzing these survey data requires the knowledge gained by experience and observation of public services staff to differentiate among various needs and uses of library resources by different user groups. When developing a library web site, the Libraries must identify <u>which</u> users' top ten list (faculty, graduate students or undergraduate students) they want to target in the structure and architecture of the site.

In addition to studying users through field studies and usability tests, the usability consultants interviewed library administrators and web developers to learn their perspectives on goals for the site, definitions of success, and barriers to success.

Usability Recommendations

The usability stage of the project yielded mountains of data. One of the most valuable contributions the usability consultants made to the IUB Libraries was the organization and documentation of this data. From the data, they issued a report with findings, noting an overly complex information structure, user difficulties with selecting appropriate resources, difficult/confusing terminology, and problems with navigation strategy. Included in their report were recommendations for solving these problems. Some of their recommendations were:

▼ Structure the site around the Top-10 most important and frequent tasks.
▼ Provide helpful descriptions of resources that people can easily read before they open the resource.
▼ Integrate searching tips throughout the web site, not just in the online help
▼ Explain key terms on the page where they are used.
▼ Notify users when they are entering a resource and leaving the IUB Libraries web site.
▼ Designate a consistent location on each page where a list of any "related links" can always be found.

In addition to the general recommendations, the usability consultants described major usability findings with supporting observations, and made specific suggestions for change.

4. Stage 2: Information Architecture

Using the data gathered from the user studies, particularly the lists of top ten tasks, the information architecture consultants performed an in-depth study of the existing web site. They met several times with the Working Group, library administrators and other groups in the Libraries to ascertain organizational ability to implement and sustain alternative structures for the site. As part of their data gathering, the consultants administered a survey to library staff and administrators asking them to name the three most important things they'd like to improve or enhance regarding the existing web site under the broad categories of "information architecture," "graphic and interface design", "content" and "functionality." The Working Group provided information on the structure of the overall site, the structure of the IUB Libraries themselves, and historical reasons for choices in the existing sites.

Information Architecture Recommendations

The information architecture consultants issued a report that listed specific and concrete short-term and long-term recommendations for the architecture and structure of a redesigned web site, including page mock-ups, menu structures, and information architecture schemes. The information architecture consultants' report included a discussion of long-term investments and actions the IUB Libraries could take to build a site easy to navigate, feasible to maintain, and that could continue to scale up in size and complexity. They suggested some actual page designs and menu constructions that could be considered for this longer-term project, and library organizational and structural changes that would have to occur to support such a project.

The information architecture consultants also strongly recommended some short-term projects; most importantly, providing interim fixes to the site's most visible and vexing problems on the "Search IUCAT/Databases" page (figure 2). Problems with this part of the site were becoming painfully obvious and had been documented in the usability studies in the first stage of this project. The consultants stated:

> "The Search IUCAT/Databases main page currently on the site is very difficult for inexperienced users to navigate—this is mostly a factor of the pull-down menus, insufficient labeling and general busy-ness of this page. The page should be re-organized so these users can view resources by subject, as well as having access to the full list of titles (linked as a separate page). Although this area of the site cannot be effectively leveraged without a behind-the-scenes database that holds all the records for the resources, the page layout can be effectively managed to make it easier for the user to find the resource they are looking for. In particular, pull-down menus might be discontinued and instead links to resources be provided. Balloon or mouse-over help can be utilized to aid users in determining the resource of their choice. To effectively determine the correct layout and help aids for this page, we recommend specific user tests with a number of alternative prototypes."

This recommendation for a behind-the-scenes database to manage this growing body of resources validated a recommendation that had been made in the IUB Libraries earlier, but had not gained sufficient internal support to be implemented.

5. Using the Consultants' Recommendations to Make Improvements

While the IUB Libraries were not in a position to create several new positions or reallocate staff to develop a new site (as suggested by the information architecture consult-

67

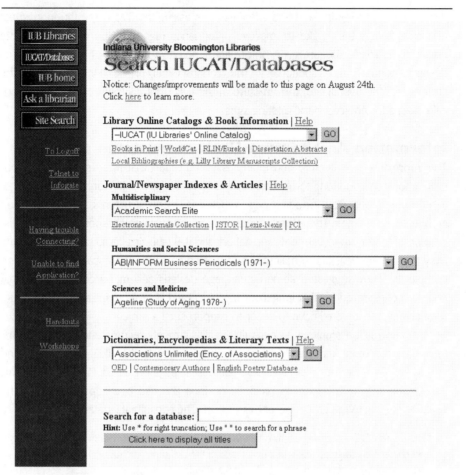

figure 2. Search Page

ants), they recognized the importance of improving the "Search IUCAT/Databases" page (from this point on to be referred to as the "Search Page"). The Search Page was designed for a much smaller collection of resources and had outgrown the original design.

This page is the gateway to most of the IUB Libraries' electronic databases, web-based periodical indexes, reference tools and the IU Libraries Catalog (IUCAT). The Search Page receives over 40,000 visits each month and is the first screen that library users see when they log into an in-library workstation. The page was documented as one of the most frequently accessed pages over the past several years, and access to "IUCAT" and other research databases consistently ranked in the top three most frequent and important tasks across all user groups.

The Libraries appointed an interim Web Coordinator and a Task Force to improve the Search Page. The Task Force included public service librarians and technology staff. Many members had also served on the Web Assessment/Evaluation Working Group that was co-chaired by the previous Web Coordinator librarian. The following is an excerpt from the charge to the Task Force to Improve the Search IUCAT/Databases Page (Task Force):

"Your charge is to review the present main page with usability results from the usability study along with the specific recommendation from the information architecture study and to suggest changes that will improve use of the site. Prototype redesigns should be tested with users. You should consult at appropriate times with the Bloomington Electronic Resources and Services Committee and with individuals who served on the expanded Working Group for the Assessment Project.... Implementation of this important work should be completed by the beginning of the fall 1999 semester."

The Task Force had about six weeks to meet the goals outlined in the charge. They reviewed the consultants' reports and extracted sections that focused on overall usability and architectural improvements and sections specific to the IUCAT/Databases Page. The usability recommendations included:

▼ Remove library jargon, where possible.
▼ Explain key terms on the page where they are used.
▼ Provide search tips for different types of searches.
▼ Provide tips for using particular resources, especially those that are most difficult or confusing.
▼ Notify users when they are entering a resource and leaving the IUB Libraries Web site.
▼ Develop a consistent navigation strategy that enables users to access the key areas of the Web site from any IUB Libraries Web site page.
▼ Designate a consistent location on each page where a list of any 'related links' can always be found.
▼ Make sure there is always a way to "Go Back".

An important factor in the redesign process was that the IUCAT/Databases page would be the sole section of the Libraries' web site to be changed. The redesign would keep the basic appearance of the template upon which the entire site was built. Due to the time constraints the Web Coordinator created the first draft prototypes. The Task Force responded to them and participated in further developments and improvements. The Web Coordinator created three paper prototypes. The design of the prototypes were based on the consultants' reports and usability test results, and they preserved the template as their design. Task Force members used the consultants' reports as well as their experience with library users to suggest changes and improvements in the prototypes. The first set of prototypes served as the starting point from which to develop improved labeling and organization of the page.

figure 3. Search Page
Paper Prototype #1

The Task Force re-worked the prototypes and continued their discussion of labeling, jargon and organization. Throughout the process the negative and positive aspects of the "old" page were discussed and comparisons were made to be certain the new page was moving toward "improvement". When possible, the Task Force made decisions using recommendations and criteria cited in literature of the field of usability and web design.

The Task Force eventually worked the three prototypes into two (figures 3 and 4), but remained divided on which of the two presented the better solution. They agreed that usability testing would be the only way to decide which to choose or which parts of the prototypes to integrate into one. Several members of the Task Force had experience in usability testing; however, no one had ever attempted to test two prototypes at the same time. They reviewed the literature and consulted with the usability expert on campus to learn how to attempt such a test. Based on the information gathered the following plan was developed.

"Each prototype will be tested on a group of representative users. Both groups will consist of one faculty instructor, one graduate student, and two undergraduate students. Each group of test participants will use the paper prototypes to accomplish the same set of tasks. The tasks will be adapted from the original usability study that the consultants conducted. At the end of each test, the participants will be asked open-ended questions about the prototype that they tested. They will also be asked to look at the prototype that they did not test and comment on it and state a preference between the two versions. After the initial testing determines a single prototype to use, a final electronic version will be tested for ease of navigation and functionality."

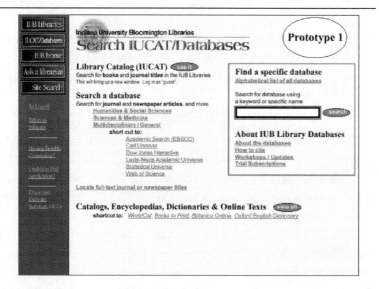

figure 3. Search Page Paper Prototype #1

figure 4. Search Page Paper Prototype #2

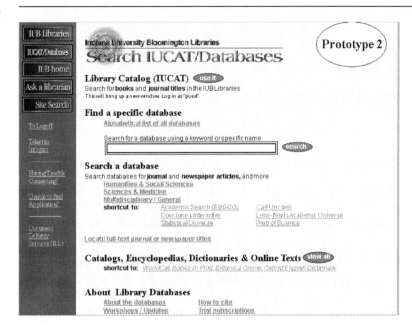

figure 4. Search Page Paper Prototype #2

The prototype tests were conducted with an observer and a note-taker and all sessions were audiotape-recorded. The test participants from each group were very similar. The faculty participants were familiar with the current Search Page and used it for their teaching as well as their research. The graduate students had similar background and experience using academic libraries and the two groups of undergraduate students included one user who was familiar with the page and one who was not.

The test participants were asked to completed the following tasks:

1. Where would you check to see if the IU Bloomington Library has a copy of the book *Catcher in the Rye*? How would you use your mouse to access it?
2. Could you access an online/electronic encyclopedia from this page? Where would you look and how would you access it?
3. You are researching about the causes of panic attacks. Where would you look to find articles on this topic? What would you do to access this information?
4. How could you find the ERIC database on this page? What would you do?
5. There is a "Newsweek" magazine article that you would like to read and you want to know if it is available in full-text. Is there a place on this page you can find that type of information? Where is it and how would you select it?
6. You need to know how to prepare a bibliographic citation for a full-text article you obtained from a database. Can you find such information on this page? How would you access it?

7. Please read through the categories on this page and tell me what you expect to find when you visit this part of the page.

8. This is another prototype we are testing. This prototype has all the same information as the one that you tested. Which of the two would you prefer to use and why?

Better terms for labeling and wording for both prototypes were discovered through usability testing. The Task Force intended to use the results from the user tests to select the better of the two prototypes. However, the prototypes produced equal test results in almost every aspect. The prototypes received almost the same number of successful responses, and length of time it took each of the participants to complete the tasks was also very close. The preferences stated by the test participants were also equal. Four participants liked the first prototype, four liked the second and there was no distinction between the user categories. The faculty each had a preference for a different prototype, as did the graduate students, as did the undergraduate students. The prototypes looked the same on Internet Explorer and Netscape. The single factor that placed one prototype above the other was that the second prototype layout adapted better to a Lynx browser than the first.

Though the Task Force chose the second prototype screen layout, all the information gathered from both prototype tests was used to improve labeling and categorization for the final screen design. For example, the category label "Research Databases & Electronic Journals: search for journal and newspaper articles" was changed to "Search a database: Search databases for journal and newspaper articles, and more". Another label change that discussions with test participants facilitated was the change from "Reference Databases & Online Texts" to "Catalogs, Encyclopedias, Dictionaries, Images & Online Texts". The Task Force did not want to lose appropriate library terminology so whenever possible more descriptive text was added to help the user understand the labels and categories. The Task Force members also learned that none of the test participants understood what they would find under the link "Trial subscriptions", they did understand the label "Databases NEW THIS SEMESTER".

The final paper prototype was made into a web page and the Task Force gathered three more users for one final round of testing: one faculty instructor, one graduate student and one undergraduate student. There were two main purposes of this final test. The first was to learn whether the navigation between the layers of the new screen design were effective. The second was to learn if the new categories and labels were clear. The final test participants were asked to complete the following tasks using the electronic version of the new prototype:

1. Where would you check to see if the IU Bloomington Library has a copy of the book *Catcher in the Rye?* Using the mouse, how would you access it?

2. Could you access and online/electronic encyclopedia from this page? Where would you look and how would you access it?

3. You are researching about the causes of panic attacks. Where would you look to find articles on this topic? What would you do to access this information?

figure 5. Search Page
Redesign

4. How could you find the ERIC database on this page? What would you do?

The final test only resulted in small changes before the final design (figure 5) was implemented. To prepare the users for the change there was a notice posted on the "old page" for one week prior to the implementation of the new design. The new design was implemented immediately before the new academic year in 1999 with little notice. The charge given to improve the layout of the Search Page was met. The screen still has many limitations and the IUB Libraries will need to find a better long-term solution. Since the revision, however, the site has endured other small changes well.

After the redesign of the Search Page, the IUB Libraries established a new position of Web Administrator. Because that position has not yet been filled, work on the redesign of the Web site is on hold. A Web Interim Team of librarians and technologists has been appointed to maintain the current site, make suggestions on policy changes and new services, and to work on projects in preparation for the new Web Administrator.

figure 5. Search Page Redesign

6. Working with Consultants: Lessons Learned

Consultants are often in a position to provide an unbiased, expert view of a situation that has become too close and familiar to people working in the institution. Consultants can bring specialized expertise, experience, and knowledge gained across institutions to identify and document known or unknown issues and solutions. They can provide data and/or expert opinions that allow an organization to "get off the dime" of internal disagreements. They can ensure neutral usability testing, a task that can be extremely difficult for people who are invested in the design and content of the site.

At the same time, librarians and library staff often possess in-depth knowledge developed from years of specialized experience and close observations of users' frustrations and triumphs. Consultants who are not experienced in working with students and faculty will not be able to bring that knowledge to their reports. In addition, consultants cannot ensure the wide internal communication that is critical to the success of a viable web site. Ideally, if a consultant is used, a knowledgeable committee of librarians and technologists should work closely with the consultant. A combination of usability expertise and library expertise can provide the best of both.

While there was certainly not 100% agreement in the Libraries with all the recommendations offered by the consultants, many of their recommendations were accepted and led to concrete actions. The project convinced library administrators that a dedicated Web Administrator position was needed. It also led to the quick redesign of the most problematic and heavily used part of the site, the "Search IUCAT/ Databases" pages.

There were intangible benefits as well:

▼ Working with experts in usability testing and information architecture was a valuable learning experience for librarians and library staff, who developed skills in conducting usability tests and learned about industry trends in information architecture.

▼ The consultants' use of a "Top-Ten List" was a very useful tool to focus the institution's attention on the categories/tasks identified by users as the most important or most frequent. Such a list is very difficult to achieve internally, always subject to questions and challenges from various user groups and perspectives. Another valuable by-product of the "Top-Ten List" was its use as a vehicle for a campus-wide survey on use of the libraries' web site.

▼ The consultants' work produced mountains of valuable use data and analyses to ensure that the redesign of the site would be done with full knowledge of user needs and difficulties.

Potential problems:

▼ The Libraries' commitment to close involvement in the process guaranteed that this would be a resource-intensive endeavor, including not only the consulting fees, but also librarians and library staff time.

74

▼ Conceived in isolation, consultants' analyses and perspectives may miss important local or content-specific issues, and result in off-base, irrelevant, or even destructive recommendations. Decision-makers must take special care to balance consultants' recommendations with expertise and knowledge in the organization itself. The IUB Libraries experience with consultants strengthened the belief that such studies must be structured to make the best use of both the consultants' and the librarians' expertise. Librarians and library staff provided input at every stage of the project: the Working Group's identified test subjects, developed typical tasks, directly observed the sessions. The library administration participated at key stages in the analyses. Broad input from throughout the libraries was made possible by various communication avenues sponsored by the Working Group.

▼ The usability studies at IUB Libraries were structured to identify problems. Most of the usability tasks were specifically chosen to explore and document known problems with the site. Decision-makers must remember that such studies, while very useful at documenting problems with a site, may not be as effective in identifying useful features that should be retained and developed further. This is much more critical in a redesign of a large site than in building one from scratch.

7. Conclusion

Outside consultants can provide libraries with expertise, objectivity and broad experience in the development of web sites. In order to gain maximum benefit from the consultants, libraries should clearly articulate the desired outcomes for the usability testing and recommendations. Clearly stated objectives help both the libraries and the consultants make recommendations that are relevant to the libraries' needs.

Working with consultants can provide significant benefits. Consultants use the data gathered about the characteristics and habits of the libraries' users to shape their recommendations for design changes and their insights on growing and sustaining complex web sites. In addition to the reports and data produced by consultants, working with consultants can provide invaluable professional development opportunities for library staff. Observing the consultants at work, participating in the design and implementation of user and field tests, learning about technical and organizational structures for web site design, observing how to structure discussions to lead to informed decisions; all are valuable experiences that can prepare the library staff to manage its web site. At IUB Libraries, library staff used the consultants' data and recommendations as well as the usability testing techniques and expertise gained from working with them to improve a key part of the web site and plan for more expansive development.

At the same time, libraries must consider the potential disadvantages of working with consultants. Most obvious, perhaps, are the costs, which include not only the consultants' fees, but also a substantial commitment of staff time and resources to fully participate in the process. This is particularly critical if consultants are not experienced with academic libraries or higher education institutions, in which case they must work very close-ly with library staff or risk misguided tests and results. At IUB Libraries, the consultants at times misjudged or misdiagnosed a problem because of inadequate understanding of the research process and the educational mission. For example, a test participant's lack of understanding of a resource or term was mistaken for a usability violation rather than a user education opportunity. Educating the consultants about the library's collections and services as well as about the library's major groups of users is key to making the assessment of the web site or library system meaningful and successful.

Libraries should be aware that consultants are very thorough in their analysis of a site or system, and working with them will require a commitment to sometimes costly analysis. The reports, plans, or recommendations that the consultants produce are helpful tools that can be used to guide a library in changes or a redesign of a web site.

WORKS CITED

Argus Associates. Architectural Framework for the IUB Libraries Web Site. 1999

Gomoll, Kate and Cathrine Spiaggia. User Research for the IUB Libraries Web site. 1999.

WORKS CONSULTED

Nielsen, Jakob "Testing Paper Mock-Up of Homepage" http://www.useit.com/papers/sun/papertest.html May 1995 (Accessed 3-19-01)

Rosenfeld, Louis and Peter Morville. Information Architecture for the World Wide Web. Sebastopol, CA: O'Reilly & Associates, 1998

Rubin, Jeffrey Handbook of Usability Testing: How to Plan, Design, and Conduct Effective Tests. New York: John Wiley & Sons, Inc., 1994.

Spool, Jared M. Web Site Usability: A Designers Guide. San Francisco: Morgan Kaufmann Publishers, 1999

Indiana University Bloomington Libraries: http://www.indiana.edu/~libweb/index.html

chapter 7

Redesigning the Information Playground

A Usability Study of the Kansas City Public Library's Web Site
David King

Beginnings...

Kansas City Public Library is an urban public library that serves the greater metropolitan Kansas City area of 1.7 million people. The library system is large, and includes nine branches and one central library. The library's web site is just as large, with over 3,000 pages and over 13,000 links.

Kansas City Public Library's current web site is a makeover of the original site. It has an attractive visual look-and-feel, and started out with a logical flow to information presented on the site. Unfortunately, through the past couple of years, when new information was added to the site, it was added without concern to the site's logical organizational structure. The end result was a large web site with over 75 links on the main page, some links repeating up to three times.

Most of the links are located in columns on the left and right hand side of the main page, and a big library news section takes up valuable space in the middle of the main page. The library's Information Technology (IT) staff knew it was time to update the look of the library's site, and decided at the same time to redesign the information flow as well. To do this, IT staff performed a usability study of the current web site as a guide to improvements that could be made.

Description of the Study
Overview of Methodology

Once IT staff decided that the current web site's usability needed to be studied in order to find possible changes and updates, an appropriate usability study method needed to

Pages viewed the most	Total for Period	Average of Period	% of Total
/default.htm	186213	1980.99	18.48
/search/srchweb.htm	77110	820.32	7.65
/docdel/onlinemagazines.htm	57731	614.16	5.73
/search/srchengines.htm	55987	595.61	5.55
/ref/default.htm	15695	166.97	1.56
/kidlinks/default.htm	15422	164.06	1.53
/query/query.idq	15137	161.03	1.50
/query/query.htm	14798	157.43	1.47
/docdel/default.htm	14344	152.60	1.42
/sc/default.htm	10194	108.45	1.01
/kidlinks/	10045	106.86	1.00
/kidlinks/ae_games.htm	9112	96.94	0.90
/search/altavista.htm	7897	84.01	0.78
/search/chart.htm	6810	72.45	0.68
/scripts/lassoisapi.dll	6729	71.59	0.67
Total for Period (4014 items)	**1007880**	**251.09**	**n/a**

table 1. LiveStats Most Popular Page Views

table 1. LiveStats Most Popular Page Views

be chosen. In the end a combination of techniques was used, including an analysis of the library's web site usage statistics, a cognitive walkthrough of the web site, and a usability test of customers and staff.

Duration of Study

The log file analysis and the cognitive walkthrough and the test questions were studied and created in June 1999. The study and analysis took place in July – August 1999. In mid-August, the study results were released to the library administration and the library staff for further comments and suggestions. The entire process took 1½ months.

Analysis of Web Site Usage Statistics

To obtain site usage statistics, IT staff gathered information from the library's public web server's log files. Kansas City Public Library uses *Statistics Server LiveStats,* a product from *MediaHouse Software* (http://www.mediahouse.com), to track usage statistics for the library's public web site. *LiveStats* tracks web log files for web sites, and creates statistics from the information found in the log files. Some statistics given include: *Pages Viewed, Most and Least Popular Pages, Dead Links, User Sessions,* and *Browser Types.*

To analyze use of the library's web site, IT staff tracked the library's 20 most popular web pages. To do this, the software allows one to choose a range of dates. March through June – all the log files that were available – were used, in order to get a broad overview of the library's most popular pages.

Using this table, the most popular pages quickly appeared:

1. Default web page
2. Search the Web – list of search engines
3. Magazines and Newspapers page
4. Introduction to Search Engines – descriptions of different search engines
5. Reference and Internet Links page
6. Youth page, especially online games
7. Search the library's web site page
8. Special Collections/local history page

A Few Observations

LiveStats doesn't track links that go from one server to another. Since the library's online library catalog is linked from the main page, but resides on another server, nothing was counted using *LiveStats.* Approximately 40,000 customers use the online library catalog each month.

Obviously, the web site's main page is a very popular page, since many links on the library's web site begin at the main page. Also, both staff and in-house library customers use the main page heavily, so the high numbers from the log files are slightly flawed.

Some of the library's pages, like the library's *Introduction to Search Engines,* are popular pages and appear often in *Yahoo* searches and are linked on other web sites, so the search engines page would appear as popular, even though it's not always reached by "traditional" means (traditional in this case meaning pages accessed through the top level page of the library's web site).

Even with the statistical problems mentioned above, examining the library's log files gave IT staff a general idea of popular pages and use. Those findings were used, along with a cognitive walkthrough of the web site, to create questions for the usability study discussed later.

Cognitive Walkthrough of the Web Site

After examining the web site's log files, IT staff performed a cognitive walkthrough of the web site. The main reason for the walkthrough was to find what IT staff considered to be important information found using the library's web site that didn't appear in the top twenty most popular web pages (a good example being the library's catalog).

The walkthrough began with the list of popular pages discussed above, and then continued with an examination of every link on the library's top-level web page. A note was made of information that was included under each link. This included areas of the library's web site that, while not included on the list of popular pages, still seemed to be important segments of the library's web site. Some of these areas included the library catalog, links to periodical databases, reader's advisory, About the Library, Friends of the Library, locations and maps of the library's branch libraries, and the library's hours of operation.

The completed walkthrough list was then combined with the list gathered from the log file analysis. This combined list became a checklist of areas to be tested during the library's formal usability study.

Usability Test of Customers and Staff

Once IT staff had gathered a list of the most popular pages and a list of pages/areas of the web site found to provide useful information, a usability study was created and implemented. This section describes the creation of the questions and the site test of both customers and library staff.

Creating Questions

Taking the information found using the analysis of the web site log files and from the library's cognitive walkthrough of the web site, IT staff created a list of areas of the web site to test. This list included: search engine links, online magazines, reference links, information under the library's About the Library link (Friends of the Library), local history pages, the youth pages, library catalog, locations and maps of branch libraries, hours of operation, Ask a Librarian email link, check-out policy, library jobs link, library databases page, and reader's links.

From this list, IT staff created 15 questions. The questions were designed with two ideas in mind: First, to test if top-level links made sense to the web site's users; and second, to test if information could be found on the next sub-level pages. For example, one of the questions asked volunteers to find information on joining the library's Friends of the Library program. This question not only tested if volunteers could find the appropriate information, but it also tested sub-level links that existed under the main page's top-level links, since the Friends of the Library page is listed underneath the top-level link, About the Library. The questionnaire can be found in Appendix A.

Site Test of Customers and Staff

Once the questionnaire was created, IT staff had to figure out how best to implement the study. According to Jakob Nielsen, testing five users is adequate (Nielsen, 2000). The library systems branches serve customers from different socio-economic backgrounds, and the central library serves a wide range of customers, from the homeless to high-level executives. Since the library has a wide range of customers, IT staff decided to use a cross section of 20 volunteers, both library staff and customers: 10 library customers and 10 library staff members, all randomly selected.

Two customers were chosen from the library's large central library, and then two-three customers from three branch libraries were chosen. Some of the branch libraries

table 2. Usability Study
Volunteers

are in more urban settings than others, so IT staff found volunteers from both the more urban branches and from the library's outlying metro area branches.

IT staff decided to test both staff and customers to get a broader view of usability. Although the impetus for the study was to find out how library customers find information using the library's web site, IT staff felt the added information about staff use of the site would also be useful.

For the library's staff volunteers, the same branches/central library sites were used. Both librarian and non-librarian staff were asked to volunteer.

To find volunteers, IT staff called ahead to the branch manager to find out when the busier, higher traffic times were – to make sure many potential volunteers were at the library. Then IT staff were positioned by the public workstations, and asked people to volunteer for the library's study. If customers chose to participate, they were given a Kansas City Public Library mouse pad.

Once a person volunteered, the volunteer and the IT staff person sat down in front of a public workstation. The volunteer was then read this statement:

"The goal of this study is to evaluate how people find information using Kansas City Public Library's website. I will ask 15 questions and would like you to think out loud while looking for the answer. I will time you, and will stop you after 3 minutes have passed. Don't worry if you can't find the answer every time – we are testing our website, not you! Each answer can be found using the library's website. The test should take no more than 20 minutes. Do you have any questions?"

After any preliminary questions were answered, the test began.

During the study, the IT staff person asked the volunteer a question, and then measured the time each question took to answer (volunteers were given three minutes to answer each question). The IT staff person also wrote down the URL of the final answer, if an answer was found, and also described the volunteer's search process – each page the volunteer went to was written down, as well as information like what the volunteer said or if the volunteer paused to read information.

CUSTOMER		LIBRARY STAFF		
Branch	**# of Volunteers**	**Branch**	**# of Staff**	**# of Librarians**
South East		South East	3	
Plaza	3	Plaza	3	
Trails West	2	Trails West	1	1
Central Library	2	Central Library	1	1

table 2. Usability Study Volunteers

Gleaning Information from the Study

Once all the usability tests were taken, a report was created using the information gleaned from the study. The report was broken into sections, including a General Summary, Customer Comments, Results and Possible Changes, Staff Comments, Results and Possible Changes, and the Questionnaire used.

The General Summary, at the beginning of the report, provided an introduction and gave a general summary of findings. The Customer section follows. It consists of a Customer Comments section, a Customer Results section, and Possible Changes. The Customer Comments section lists each question and the number of correct/incorrect answers to the question. A discussion follows describing what each volunteer did while trying to answer the question. A brief conclusion accompanies each question, and summarizes the information found for that question, including changes that might need to be made to the area covered by the question, or if links covered under the question seem to make logical sense to the volunteers. The Customer Results section lists each question again. Listed with each question are the paths each volunteer took while trying to answer the questions. The Possible Changes section is a summary of each of the conclusions from the Customer Comments part of the report. The Staff section mimics the Customer section. The questionnaire used ends the report.

Gathering the information found during the study into a concise report provided a wealth of information. IT staff were quickly able to see which questions volunteers were able to answer, and which questions volunteers had trouble with and why, judging from the paths taken when attempting to answer the questions.

What We Learned from the Study

IT staff gathered much useful information during this study. Table 3 shows which questions were answered correctly (yes), incorrectly (no). Questions that volunteers were not able to answer in the three minute time allotment were also counted as incorrect (no) answers. Some questions underneath the Customer section are marked as "N/A." One customer volunteered for the study, and then had to leave before completing the study.

Using the usability study answers as a guide, IT staff created a partial list of potential changes that needed to be made to the library's web site:

1. Some top-level links needed to be renamed. Many customers didn't know that clicking "Online Catalog" would lead to the library's online library catalog. The word "Online" should be dropped, and the word "library" should be added to the link text to make the link less confusing.
2. Links under some major headings, like "Reference and Internet Links" and "About the Library," were not readily apparent to customers. Re-designing the top-level page or renaming the top-level links might help the information be easier to access.

table 3. Answers to Usability
Test Questions

3. The library's News section was taking up valuable space in the middle of the main page. Our volunteers seemed to get confused by seeing, and thinking they needed to read, the summaries of news items.
4. Some top-level links were hard to find because volunteers had to scroll down the browser's screen to find the link (they didn't scroll).
5. Librarian/technical terminology like Policy, Reference, Borrower, and Online were confusing to volunteers.
6. IT staff discovered that the volunteers scanned pages starting with the upper left-hand corner of the screen, then scanned down the screen, and then did the same for the right-hand side of the screen. Some of the library's important links are located on the right-hand side of the page, and were missed by volunteers – they sometimes chose incorrect links on the left-hand side of the page, rather than scanning the right-hand side of the page before choosing a link.
7. Information should be linked on more than one page, when possible (example: video pages could be linked on the top-level page and also linked on a movie resource page). At the same time, there should be no more than one link to a resource per page (there are currently three links to the library catalog on the library's main page – and volunteers still couldn't find the library catalog!).

CUSTOMER				STAFF		
#	Yes	No	N/A	#	Yes	No
1.	6	4		1.	9	1
2.	4	6		2.	5	5
3.	2	8		3.	9	1
4.	2	8		4.	7	3
5.	5	5		5.	9	1
6.	6	4		6.	10	0
7.	2	7	1	7.	10	0
8.	4	5	1	8.	9	1
9.	7	2	1	9.	9	1
10.	2	7	1	10.	5	5
11.	6	3	1	11.	6	4
12.	1	8	1	12.	8	2
13.	6	3	1	13.	9	1
14.	6	3	1	14.	5	5
15.	4	5	1	15.	9	1

table 3. Answers to Usability Test Questions

8. Volunteers didn't find links that were side-by-side in a vertical list of links. For example, the library's page has two links, Locations and Hours, side by side, rather than under or above each other. Volunteers didn't see the second link (Hours) as easily.

9. The library's current web site has links on the main page, a shortcuts drop down list, an index of the site, and a "Search this Web Site" feature. In some cases this provided four links to the same information. This aspect confused some volunteers. If the site's information flow is logical, there's no need to provide 4-5 links to information on the same page.

10. The library's video page had an image map at the top of the page with five links to further information about videos at the library. But the font used when creating the image was difficult to read, and confused some volunteers.

11. Links to library periodical databases needed to be included with links on subject reference pages. The library's customers would be served better if those links were combined on one subject page – hence all the internet links and library databases for individual subjects can all be found on one page rather than two.

12. Pages that provide lists of new books and videos should also link, or at least point to, the library catalog. More than once, a volunteer tried to see if the library owned a video by checking out the library's video pages, which describe new videos and provide links to movie-related web sites.

13. The library's Friends of the Library pages were hidden to most volunteers. The library's fundraising pages needed to be placed in a higher-traffic area of the web site.

Some interesting discoveries also stemmed from using both library customers and library staff for the study. What IT staff discovered from the customer study was interesting, but not surprising (in some cases, anyway). But results from the library staff study showed that more training would be useful to library employees, especially the library's lower-level, para-professional staff.

Changes...
After completing this study, IT staff redesigned the library's web site. Both a new visual look and a new information architecture, or information flow, were designed. Some drastic changes were made to the web site, both in terms of design and information flow.

Design
The look-and-feel of the web site has been redesigned, both with an eye to the results of the library's usability study, and to current web site design trends. For example, white space has been added to give more room for visitors to see and read the text presented on the page. All the links fit on one screen, rather than requiring the web site visitor to scroll down to find more links. The News and Events section has been moved to the less-important, right-hand side of the top-level page, and given a brief sentence with a link to more information.

The new web site will have movement on its pages, too. There are plans to have rotating banner ads (discussed below) and images that change each time the page is refreshed. There will also be mouse over links that pull up a description of what can be found underneath the highlighted link.

Information Flow

The number of links found on the library's main page has been whittled down from a whopping 78 (including two to four news items that change each month and a drop down list of short cuts) to a much more manageable 15-17 links, divided into five areas:

1. Library Links: There are four main links that contain all the usual library-related information, like the library's catalog, reference links, reader's advisory, about the library, and the youth area. Librarian and "techie" terms were removed in link text, when possible (for example, reference links and periodical databases are both included under Resources, a top-level link). These links are located in the top left section of the page. The link text (actually an image) is visually large, and stands out a little more than other links on the page. A visual mouse over describing what can be found under each top-level link is provided, which will help the customer choose an appropriate link. These four "Library Links" also appear in the header section on all sub-level pages.

2. Housekeeping Links: These links also appear on every page, in the page's footer section. Included here are links like My Account, Contact us, Ask a Librarian, Search the Web Site and Help. These links, while important to the operation of a web site, aren't among the library's most important resources, and therefore are included in the footer of the main page and have a smaller font.

3. Fund Raising Banner Ad: This will provide the library's marketing department with a good way to highlight library events and fundraisers. The banner ad is planned to be displayed in the header of every page of the library's web site. It will be able to rotate, so that the banner image and link to more information will change when the page refreshes.

4. News and Events: The News section is now located on the right-hand side of the main page. Each news item now gets a small line of small-font text, which will link to the full story. Plans are to place this information in a database, so that news can be updated on-the-fly.

5. Service/Resource Feature: A graphic in the middle of the page links to an in-depth feature on a unique service, new resource, or an innovative program of the library. It will also rotate when the page is refreshed, so more than one service can be highlighted.

The biggest change to the web site is in its focus. The old web site was very staff/departmental focused – links lead to departments of the library, rather than to specific resources.

The new site will be customer-focused. Wording has been changed so that the library's customers will be able to understand what they've found, rather than finding wording created by and for librarians. Links have been removed from departmental compartments, and have been placed in more logical groupings (the biggest grouping being Resources). The end result should be an information-rich web site that serves as a virtual one-stop shop for the library's customers.

WORKS CITED

Nielsen, Jakob. "Why You Only Need to Test With 5 Users." Jakob Nielsen's Alertbox, March 19, 2000. http://www.useit.com/alertbox/20000319.html, Accessed 12/2/00.

Kansas City Public Library: http://www.kclibrary.org/

APPENDIX A.
Usability Study Questions

Public Website Usability Study Questionnaire
Administered by:
Date:
Read to Volunteer:

The goal of this study is to evaluate how people find information using Kansas City Public Library's website. I will ask 15 questions and would like you to think out loud while looking for the answer. I will time you, and will stop you after 3 minutes have passed. Don't worry if you can't find the answer every time – we are testing the library's website, not you! Each answer can be found using the library's website. The test should take no more than 20 minutes. Do you have any questions?

Usability Questions:

1. You want to use the Google search engine to search the Internet for information on cars. Can you find Google using the library's website?
2. Is the Missouri Conservationist, an online magazine, linked on the library's website?
3. You need to find a definition for the word "frenzy." Where do you go to find the definition?
4. You want more information on becoming a Friend of the library. Where do you find this information?
5. A friend mentioned that the library has an online postcard collection, and you want to see it for yourself. Where do you go to find this collection?
6. Your daughter's grades are slipping, and she needs help with her homework. Does the library have a website that will help her?
7. Does the library have a copy of the 1954 movie, *Rear Window*?
8. You want to drive to the North East branch library, and need to find directions. Can you find them using the library's website?
9. You have a burning desire to read a book on Memorial Day. Is the library open?
10. You're at work, and have a question you want help with. You have Internet access, but can't use your phone. Where do you go to ask a question online?
p 11. You want to know how long you can check out a movie. Where is that information located?
12. Where do you find historical information about the library?
13. You have a friend who wants to work for the library, and needs the library's jobline phone number. Where is the number located?
14. Is the Art Index one of the library's databases?
15. You've heard that Oprah has a book club. Can you find a link to it on the library's website?

chapter 8

Card-sorting Usability Tests of the MIT Libraries' Web Site

Categories from the Users' Point of View

Nicole Hennig

I. Introduction

In March of 1999 we conducted a usability test of our web site (the web site for all of the libraries at MIT). This was an observed test where 30 users from different groups who use our site, e.g., undergraduates, graduate students, faculty, staff, alumni, etc., were asked to find the answers to specific questions while thinking out loud about what they were clicking on and why. We did this to prepare for redesigning our site; so that we could better understand exactly which aspects of it worked and didn't work for our users. Detailed results are available in a report on our staff web site.[1]

The MIT Libraries are distributed throughout the campus, but have a centralized administrative office and collection/technical services department. The web site[2] serves as a unified presence to describe the libraries' services, and there are also individual home pages for each of the 13 libraries on campus. These are sub-sites related to the site as a whole, with the same graphic design.

One of the major problems we saw during the test mentioned above was that our category names were too broad, and therefore not helpful to people navigating our site. Some examples were "Resources," "Services," and "Subjects." Another problem was that our web site was mapped to the physical world of our library system. For example, in addition to these broad categories, the other prominent links on our home page were the names of the individual libraries on our campus. We felt that we weren't taking best advantage of the web as a medium where it's possible to present a unified set of tools

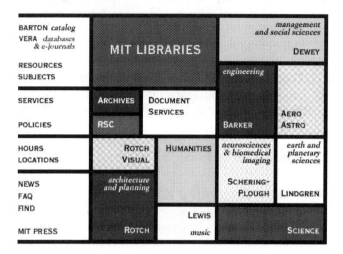

Copyright © Massachusetts Institute of Technology
webmaster@libraries.mit.edu

figure 1. MIT Libraries' Home Page before Redesign

89

and services for our users. The users should not have to know which library on campus published the information they were looking for in order to navigate the site.

So in order to help us begin to group the information on our site in a new way, we conducted a set of card-sorting tests in the summer of 1999. The inspiration for these tests was an article by Fuccella and Pizzolato (Fuccella 1998).[3] These tests helped us determine what the new broad categories of our site should be.

II. Purpose of the test and method overview

The purpose of this kind of test is to find out how our users would group the information on our site into categories. This test is not so much to find out the exact names people use to describe things, but to find out if there are similarities in how our users mentally group the information in ways that are meaningful to them.

The basic method of this test is described in general terms below.

Part A – Card sorting

1. Make a list of actual link names from many different pages of your site, i.e. "research assistance," or "library photocopiers."
2. Print them out on labels and attach them to index cards.
3. Make several duplicate sets of these cards.
4. Take one set and shuffle it in random order.
5. Have one of your staff meet individually with volunteers who are users of your site.

6. Ask them to sort the cards into categories that make sense to them. A large table in a conference room is ideal for this activity so that there is room to spread out the cards.
7. Ask them to make up a name for each category, write it on a sticky note, and attach one to each pile of cards.
8. Collect the card sets from each volunteer that has done this.
9. Look for similarities in the categories that that the volunteers created and record the general concepts or terminology that they used (ignore the idiosyncratic or unusual things that only one person did).
10. Use the concepts and terms that emerge to help you decide what new category names to use.

Part B – Category description

1. In order to test whether the categories you chose make sense to people, create a survey (may be a web form).
2. In the survey give the users each new category name and ask them to describe in a few sentences what sort of information they would expect to find in that category.
3. Use the results of this test to refine and perhaps re-word your category names.

Part C – Reverse category description

1. In order to test your revised category names, create a survey (may be a web form).
2. In the survey ask users, "which of the following categories would you click on first to find "[insert name of item here]?"
3. Repeat this question for several different items on your site (using the same category names each time).
4. Look at the results to see whether users chose the category where you were planning to list that item.
5. By this point, your ideas should be fairly well in agreement with your users' ideas about which categories contain which items. Where a significant minority disagree, you might decide to cross-reference the item in a second category.

III – How we applied this method
Details of the test – part A

1. Preparing the cards.
We chose 106 link names from several important pages on our site. Since some of them were not clear out of the context of the page, we added a few words where necessary. For example, "annual reports" became "annual reports of the MIT libraries" to distinguish it from information about how to obtain annual reports of companies. We also added some link names for content that didn't exist yet on our site, but that we planned to add, since we wanted to find out how users would group those items as well. We printed these out on label sets, which we then affixed to index cards. We made 10 sets of these cards, all with the same 100 items.

2. Recruiting volunteers

We emailed all the participants who had participated in a previous usability test and also created sign-up sheets for volunteers that we placed at circulation desks of several libraries. We explained to users that their input would help us design a better web site, and that they would receive a coupon for a free ice-cream at everyone's favorite campus ice cream shop.

We ended up with 10 volunteers, all of them students. We decided to focus on students for this test, since they are our primary audience (instead of faculty, staff, outside users, etc.)

Our Web Advisory Group (which consists of 4 library staff members plus the library web manager) conducted the test. Each of us tested 2 volunteers, except for 1 person who tested only 1 since the 2nd person did not come to the appointment. So the total number of people tested was 9. (Parts B & C used larger numbers of volunteers).

Each of us emailed our 2 volunteers to set up a 1/2-hour appointment with them. We gave ourselves a two-week period in which to conduct the two tests. At the end of that period we scheduled a meeting to compile and share our results with each other.

3. The test

Here are the materials we used for each test session:

▼ set of 106 cards with link names
▼ some extra blank cards
▼ pen
▼ rubber bands
▼ post-it notes

To prepare, we shuffled the deck so the cards were in a random order. We meet with the volunteer in a conference room at a large table with plenty of room to spread the cards out.

We read the following instructions to the volunteer at the beginning of the test:

This test is designed to help us gain some understanding of how our web site users would name the categories of information on our site. This set of cards represents some names of current content from our site as well as some possible future content that we haven't developed yet.

Take these cards and put them into piles representing categories of information that make sense to you. You may make as many or as few categories as you like.

When they are sorted, put a post-it note on top of each pile and write a name for that category on it. The name can be as long and descriptive as you like, we just want to get a sense of why you consider those links to be a group - the name doesn't have to be perfect.

The whole test should take about 1/2 hour. I have some other work or reading I can do while you're sorting, so I won't be looking over your shoulder, but feel free to ask me questions at any time.

We also decided upon the following answers to questions they might have:

1. What if I have no idea what a link name represents?
Feel free to set aside cards that have no meaning for you and leave them out of the exercise.

2. May I put cards in more than one category?
Yes. Make an extra card by copying the name on one of the blank cards and put one card in each category. Make a note on the card that says "also in [category x]."

3. I have some ideas for related or new content that I'd like to see on your site. May I include those somehow?
Yes, just use the blank cards to make up new links of your own choosing and add them to the piles.

4. What if some of the links don't seem to fit into any category?
Feel free to make a category called "other" or "general."

5. Are you really going to allow off-campus access to databases? (Or a similar question from a link name for something we don't have yet)
Some of these items are from ideas that people gave us for what they would like to see on our site. We haven't made final decisions yet about all the content we will include, but we would love to get your input about which features are most important to you.

When they were done, we put a rubber band around each labeled pile and then a rubber band around the whole set. We recorded the name and email address of each user and kept it with the card set. We brought these sets to our follow-up meeting for comparing the results.

We then thanked the volunteer for participating and gave them the coupon for a free ice cream.

4. The results

At the meeting for compiling the results, the five of us took turns describing how each test went. We gathered around a large table, took a set of cards and placed them on the table in the sets that the user chose. We told each other what the user said, which cards they set aside, and any other comments they had.

For each subsequent set of cards (representing one user's results), we placed them on top of or near similar concepts that previous users used. We placed them in an empty location on the table if it was the first time that concept was used. As we added more card sets, the table became filled up with lots of piles and categories. We continually discussed which ones represented the same concept or related concepts and moved piles around a bit until we could see the similarities in what more than one user was thinking.

At one point, one of us stepped aside to take notes on the whole process. By the end we came up with the following "summary of trends:"

Here are some of the major categories that more than one person came up with: (in no particular order)

Thesis information

links to items having to do with thesis preparation from all over our site, style guides, our e-thesis collection, ordering MIT theses, etc.

Information by Course

links to subject info, e-reserves, etc., organized by MIT Course

New materials & library news

links to anything about new books, journals, databases, etc., and library news

Ordering materials

how to order materials, whether from doc services, interlibrary borrowing, theses, etc. (whether it cost money or not) - anything to do with ordering things was grouped together

Access policies for our library and other libraries

all the links having to do with various outside groups using our libraries, and our community using other libraries

About the MIT Libraries

people put all sorts of general info in a category like this, having to do with policies, services, hours, locations, etc.

Services

many people used this word to describe links about library services and library instruction

Materials/Content/Collections

these were some terms used to describe links about our collections and physical items (including equipment) in the libraries

Reference

links that had to do with asking reference questions, virtual reference, or reference desk hours were grouped here

Databases

people used this word to mean many different things, a much broader definition of it than we usually think of (no clear trend other than this)

Note: No one used the term, "resources," to describe anything.

One thing we all noticed was that 106 cards was too many for most people to sort in 1/2 hour. We felt that 1/2 hour was about the right amount of time, and if we were to do it again we would reduce the number of cards to about 50 (or even less). We were tempted at the beginning to include so much, because we have so much content on our site and we wanted to test all of it! However, we could learn enough if we used representative content, rather than trying to include so much.

Each user had a different approach (depending on their personality) – some were very intent on telling us exactly how our web site should be organized, some were shy, some were frustrated that they couldn't finish, some were disappointed that we were using cards and not sitting in front of a computer screen. As in previous usability tests we had to reassure the volunteers that we were not testing them, but were testing our site.

5. How we applied the results

One thing the results helped us with, was noticing items that should be grouped together on a web page, that previously were scattered throughout the site. The primary example here was thesis information. Because different departments authored this information, the information was found on several different sections of our site. Of course it made perfect sense from the students' point of view to have one page that guides you to everything about theses. So we created a new page that brought every aspect of theses together and linked to the places where it was found. For example:

MIT Theses:

Identify, borrow or access an <u>MIT thesis</u>
<u>Purchase an MIT thesis</u> (Document Services)
Specifications for Thesis Preparation <u>(Institute Archives)</u>
<u>Submitting an electronic thesis</u> | You may submit your thesis electronically to <u>MIT Theses Online.</u>

Non-MIT Theses:

Identify, borrow or purchase a <u>non-MIT thesis</u>

We then set about deciding on the new top-level categories for our site. Our first draft was very rough, and not in any particular order – here is what we came up with:

▼ About the Libraries
▼ Searchable Resources
▼ Services
▼ Library News & Updates
▼ Library Information for Students, Faculty, Staff, Alumni, Visiting Researchers, non-MIT users, etc.
▼ Course-Related Information
▼ Information by Subject

As you can see above we couldn't agree on what the pages for specific audiences should be called, so we just listed them in the category name above.

figure 2. Category Survey

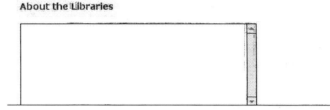

New web site categories:

**Help us decide if these categories
mean to you what they mean to us!**

For each category name below, imagine it as a link on our web site home page. For each
one:

- give a brief description of the type of information you think would be there when
  you click on it
- give a few examples of specific things you would expect to find in that section of
  our site

Your feedback will help us choose meaningful and descriptive category names for our
new web site. Thank you!

About the Libraries

figure 2. Category Survey

Details of the test – part B

1. The test
The next part of the test involved testing our first draft of category names. We created
a survey[5] as a web form that was sent out to 84 users of our site (previous volunteers
were all included, whether they had actually participated or not in our previous tests).

The survey asked users to describe what they thought would be found in each category. The seven categories we chose (listed above) were included, each with a large
text box after it for their description.

2. The results
We received 20 responses from the 84 people we sent the survey to. The following categories contained responses that matched what we were planning to put in them:

About the Libraries
Searchable Resources
Services
Library News & Updates

The following categories did not, and received a range of responses as to what users
thought they meant:

Library Information for Students, Faculty, Staff, Alumni, Visiting Researchers, non-MIT users, etc.
Course-Related Information
Information by Subject

Obviously, the information grouped by audience was an awkward one, so we removed it and planned to deal with it separately later. We found that students at MIT tend to think in terms of "courses" rather than subjects, but that the subject-related information was very much related to course information, so we combined that category into one new one, called:

Subject/Course-related Information

So our new list of top-level categories became this:

About the Libraries
Searchable Resources
Services
Library News & Updates
Subject/Course-related Information

As you can see, at this point, the wording was still a bit awkward, and is not the final exact wording we ended up with, but the concepts for what's grouped together are there. This test focuses more on concepts and how users group related material and not so much on the exact names for things.

Details of the test – part C

1. The test

Part C of the test is what we refer to as a "reverse category survey." This survey[6] takes lists specific items on our web site and asks which of our five categories they would click on first to find the information.

In this survey we asked the same question for ten different items on our site. It was sent to 84 users and we received 21 responses. This part of the test included 2 undergraduate students, 6 graduate students, 3 faculty, 3 staff, 3 alumni, and 4 MIT library staff (since we are also users of our own site).

The results[7] were encouraging, because the vast majority of responses were the exact same category where we planned to list the item. In a couple of cases where significant minorities of responses were different, we planned to cross-reference the item in that secondary category.

Conclusions

We found card-sorting tests to be very valuable in understanding our users' point of view when it comes to grouping content on our site. Since we had already conducted a

***figure 3.** Reverse Category Survey*

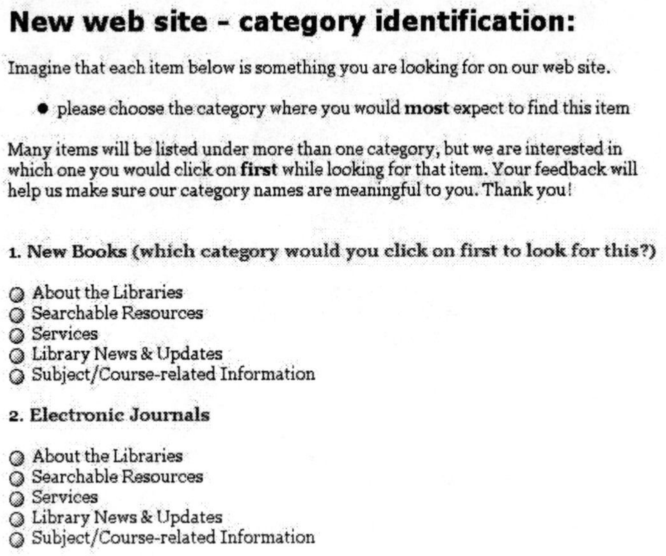

New web site – category identification:

Imagine that each item below is something you are looking for on our web site.

● please choose the category where you would **most** expect to find this item

Many items will be listed under more than one category, but we are interested in which one you would click on **first** while looking for that item. Your feedback will help us make sure our category names are meaningful to you. Thank you!

1. New Books (which category would you click on first to look for this?)

○ About the Libraries
○ Searchable Resources
○ Services
○ Library News & Updates
○ Subject/Course-related Information

2. Electronic Journals

○ About the Libraries
○ Searchable Resources
○ Services
○ Library News & Updates
○ Subject/Course-related Information

figure 3. Reverse Category Survey

traditional usability test where users were given specific tasks and asked to think out loud while being observed, this was a helpful complement to that.

Observed usability testing is great for discovering what aspects of your site are causing problems for people, but it doesn't quite give you enough information about what to do to fix the problems you observe. Card sorting does this. It helps you to move away from the "librarian" point of view, and look at things from the users' point of view.

These tests were conducted in the summer and fall of 1999. After completing them we spent nine months developing a database-backed web site for listing our electronic databases & e-journals.[8] That task was a priority because our usability tests and a survey we conducted showed that users found our listings of databases & e-journals to be our most valuable content, but there were many usability problems on these pages.

After the database-backed part of our web site was completed, it took almost another year to work on redesigning the rest of the site. As of this writing, the new site is not yet live. We hope to make it live sometime in the summer of 2001. Information about the entire process is available on our web site.[9]

We have revised the category names slightly from the final names in the test mentioned above. Here are the new category names:

Search Our Collections
Research Help
Subjects + Courses
Borrowing + Ordering
About Us

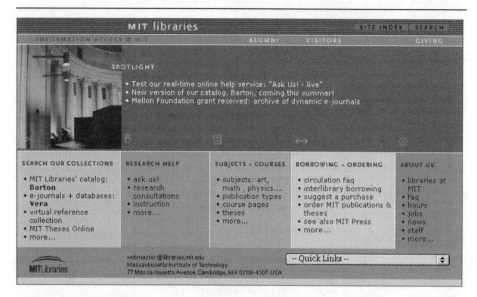

figure 4. A Draft Version of
MIT Libraries' New Home
Page

figure 4. A Draft Version of MIT Libraries' New Home Page

"Search Our Collections" came about because "searchable resources" was awkward. It's the category that contains our catalog, our database of electronic resources, and other searchable databases, such as the Digital Thesis Library.

We decided also that "Services" was still too broad, even though it was a word that many students used in the card sorting. (We guessed that this might have been because many of our link names contained the word "service" in them.) When we looked at all the content that was in our "services" section, it seemed clear that it could be divided into two categories:

Research Help
Borrowing + Ordering

The word "ordering" was the word that many students used to describe services such as interlibrary loan, purchasing MIT theses and documents (for outside users), requesting delivery of books from off-site storage, and similar items.

"Subject/Course-Related Information" became "Subjects + Courses" in order to make in more concise and to allow it to fit on a button in the navigation bar. "About the Libraries" became "About Us," partly to allow it to fit on a button and also because everything we've learned about writing style for the web indicates that speaking in the active voice and in the first person works well on web sites. [10]

These latest versions of the names will be tested again when we do more usability tests of our new web site during a preview period before we release it. We will then fix any more problems that appear before we release the final site in summer 2001.

Figure 4 is a draft of the new home page.

As you can see, the card sorting helped us to determine how users mentally group the material on our site. We highly recommend it to others as a valuable technique to use in conjunction with other types of usability tests.

FOOTNOTES

1. Previous usability test results (March 1999): http://macfadden.mit.edu:9500/webgroup/usability/results/

2. MIT Libraries' web site: http://libraries.mit.edu

3. "Creating Web Site Designs Based on User Expectations and Feedback." Jeanette Fuccella and Jack Pizzolato, IBM Corporation. Internetworking, June 1998, vol. 1.1, http://www.sandia.gov/itg/newsletter/june98/web_design.html

4. The complete list of card names: http://macfadden.mit.edu:9500/webgroup/cards/cards.html

5. Category survey: http://madfadden.mit.edu:9500/webgroup/cards/categories.html

6. Reverse category survey: http://macfadden.mit.edu:9500/webgroup/cards/category-identification.html

7. The detailed results: http://macfadden.mit.edu:9500/webgroup/cards/category2results.html

8. Our database-backed web site for listing electronic journals and databases is called "Vera: Virtual Electronic Resources Access." See, "Building a Database-Backed Web Site for E-Journals and Databases at the MIT Libraries: The Vera Project," by Nicole Hennig, forthcoming in a future issue of *Serials Librarian* (early 2002) and available on the author's web site: http://www.hennigweb.com/publications/vera.html

9. Web site redesign process: http://macfadden.mit.edu:9500/webgroup/project.html

10. Writing for the Web: Guidelines for MIT Libraries: http://macfadden.mit.edu:9500/webgroup/writing/

chapter 9

Designing a Usable Health Information Portal

The MEDLINEplus Experience from the National Library of Medicine
Jennifer L. Marill

About the National Library of Medicine

The National Library of Medicine (NLM), on the campus of the National Institutes of Health (NIH) in Bethesda, Maryland, is the world's largest medical library. The Library collects materials in all areas of biomedicine and health care, and provides access via the World Wide Web to MEDLINE and many other specialized databases. MEDLINE has more than 11 million journal article references and abstracts, and is used by health professionals, scientists, librarians, and the public. In 1998, NLM created a new Web site, MEDLINEplus (medlineplus.gov), to link the general public to many sources of consumer health information.

What NLM Studied and Why

MEDLINEplus is a portal to authoritative health information from the NIH, other federal government organizations, professional societies and voluntary health organizations. It also integrates reliable content from commercial vendors. MEDLINEplus builds on NLM strengths of selecting and organizing medical information.[1] The site is a selective collection of links to full-text publications produced by the NIH Institutes, federal government agencies and dependable educational, non-profit and for-profit organizations.

MEDLINEplus was released to the general public in October 1998, marking NLM's first substantial foray into providing consumer health information. Use of the site has grown tremendously, from 116,000 hits a month in November 1998 to over five million hits a month in February 2001. A CyberDialogue 2000 Health Portal Study (conducted in August 2000) showed that most consumers, when evaluating a health content site, consider the technical aspects of the site such as ease of navigation or a published privacy policy to be very important (Cyber Dialogue, 2000). The Study concluded that web health sites had considerable room for improvement in the navigation, depth, quantity and quality of information. The Study confirmed NLM's recognition that additional growth and outreach of MEDLINEplus could occur only if the site was reliable, authoritative, and just as importantly, easy to use. NLM has therefore embarked on a series of usability studies with the aim of improving all aspects of the site.

Usability Assessment of MEDLINEplus

In the summer of 1999, NLM contracted with the University of Maryland Human-Computer Interaction Laboratory for a MEDLINEplus interface evaluation. The evaluation comprised two phases; 1) a heuristic evaluation and 2) usability testing with nine participants. The heuristic evaluation identified interface problems of a general nature, while the usability testing highlighted specific areas of concern (Cogdill, 1999). NLM staff conducted additional usability tests in December 1999, April 2000 and May 2000. The methodology used for these three additional tests closely replicated the methodology used by the University of Maryland in the original study. This case study will describe the methodology of usability testing used at NLM and highlight major results from the testing.

Methodology of NLM Usability Testing

The three usability tests performed by NLM consisted of the following phases:

▼ Recruitment
▼ Introduction to Testing
▼ Testing
▼ Test Feedback and Post-Test Questionnaire
▼ Test Analysis

An administrator conducted each test and was generally responsible for the testing portion and analysis. All participants were videotaped and in most cases, the administrator transcribed the videotape. The videotaping (consisting of a video camera and cameraman) was contracted with an outside company. In the future, NLM will conduct usability tests using NLM owned hardware that can capture both the computer screen and audio portion.

Recruitment

Each test was performed with either five or six volunteer participants. Most participants were Federal government employees from NLM or other NIH Institutes. The participants ranged in age from the 20's to 60's and represented "typical" consumers looking for health information on the Web. The participants exhibited a range of experiences and occupations: clerical, professional, scientific, English and non-native English speakers, etc. None of the participants had previous MEDLINEplus experience.

Introduction to Testing

The administrator asked each participant to read a description of the test's purpose and format, and sign an informed consent form stating they would be videotaped. Participants also read the MEDLINEplus "Selection Guidelines" which explains MEDLINEplus' purpose and criteria for linked content to the site. Finally, participants completed brief written questionnaires to capture general demographic information.

Testing

Each participant was scheduled for an hour of testing. The participants were given up to five minutes to explore MEDLINEplus and ask any remaining questions about it. The video camera captured the participants' voices and computer screens from the start of the testing session. The administrator gave each of the participants up to 7 questions or tasks [see sidebar], and the participant had approximately 10-15 minutes to find the answer to each question. In all three usability tests, the same 7 tasks were administered. In some cases, due to a lack of time, participants were only able to answer 4-5 questions.

Test Feedback and Post-Test Questionnaire

After the participants were finished with the specific tasks, the administrator asked them general, informal questions about their experience using MEDLINEplus. The feedback was captured on the audio portion of the videotape. The participants were also asked to comment on and compare two new prototype (i.e., not "live") MEDLINEplus home pages. Finally, each participant completed a questionnaire and the results of the questionnaires were compared to each other for analysis.

Test Analysis

The administrator was responsible for analyzing his/her written notes taken during the sessions and the corresponding video clips. In most cases, the administrator compiled a report containing the following information:

▼ an executive summary;
▼ a demographic overview of each user (based on the initial written questionnaire the participant filled out);
▼ searching, browsing and other characteristics and observations of each participant's session;

Usability Tasks

▼ Find information about whether a dark bump on your shoulder might be skin cancer.
▼ Find information about whether it's safe to take Prozac during pregnancy.
▼ Find information about whether there is a vaccine for hepatitis C.
▼ Find recommendations about the treatment of breast cancer, specifically, the use of mastectomies.
▼ Find information about the dangers associated with drinking alcohol during pregnancy.
▼ Find the address of Suburban Hospital in Bethesda, Maryland.
▼ Find a doctor who specializes in pediatrics in Peoria, Illinois.

figure 1. Original MEDLINEplus Home page

figure 1. Original MEDLINEplus Home page

▼ the number of minutes each participant took to complete a task;

▼ results of the post-test questionnaire; and

▼ appendices including the usability test questions, consent form, etc.

Usability Test Findings

Analysis of the usability testing focused on two major areas of the MEDLINEplus Web site: the home page and the health topic pages. The health topic pages (e.g., breast cancer, diabetes, nutrition, etc.) are the core of MEDLINEplus. These pages pull together selected links to full-text resources, preformulated MEDLINE searches, links to clinical trials and other material. There are now over 440 topics on the site.

The following items highlight the problems and issues found on the original Home page during usability testing:

▼ New content and resources were being added to the sidebar more quickly than expected. Users often failed to see the individual categories the sidebar offered. In addition, the one- or two-word sidebar category didn't adequately explain what the user could expect on the next page.

▼ The site emphasized searching for health topics. NLM wanted to equally emphasize new resources such as drug and dictionary information.

▼ NLM needed a more prominent place to add and highlight the latest health news stories.

figure 2. Redesigned MEDLINEplus Home page

figure 2. Redesigned MEDLINEplus Home page

▼ The site had no prominent search feature (i.e., a search box) although users repeatedly asked for it.

Based on the findings above, the following improvements were made to the Home page:

▼ The page follows a grid pattern making it easier to scan.
▼ Most important and heavily used categories (i.e., health topics and drug information) are prominently displayed in the top left.
▼ Categories are now clearly labeled so users have a better understanding of what to expect on the next page.
▼ Current health news items are now featured in the top right.
▼ A search box has been added to the top of every page.
▼ Graphics provide greater visual interest (file sizes are kept as small as possible).

Usability testing identified a number of serious problems with the health topic pages:

▼ The most important content (links to full-text resources) was not positioned at the top. Users kept clicking on the Related categories and looping through the site.
▼ The horizontal bar under Table of contents acted as a "scroll stopper," discouraging exploration of the page.

figure 3. Original
MEDLINEplus Health Topic
Page

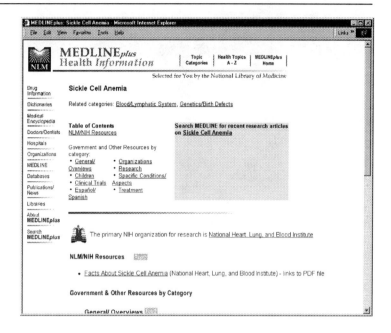

figure 3. Original MEDLINEplus Health Topic Page

▼ The preformulated MEDLINE searches were so visible that users were instantly drawn to them. Once in MEDLINE (PubMed), most users complained the resulting citations were too technical.

▼ Too much white space was devoted to the Table of contents pushing the linked content further down the page.

NLM produced a number of health topic page prototypes before settling on the layout in figure 4. This page was particularly difficult to redesign because its purpose is to pull together so many different resources related to the topic. Subsequent usability testing has proven that users can now more readily access the linked full-text content:

▼ Moved important content links to top of page and repositioned Table of contents on left side.

▼ Preformulated MEDLINE searches and Related categories/pages moved to left side, minimizing their prominence.

▼ Added ability to navigate other health topics directly from each health topic page.

▼ Moved all global site navigation to top of page.

Other Specific Comments about MEDLINEplus Findings

▼ Medical terminology is both difficult to spell and comprehend. Users can benefit from extensive spelling assistance and many testers requested a quick and easy

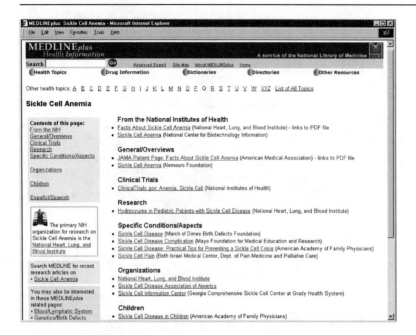

figure 4. Redesigned MEDLINEplus Helath Topic Page

figure 4. Redesigned MEDLINEplus Helath TopicPage

dictionary lookup. Technical terms should be mapped to consumer health vocabulary as much as possible and testers appreciated the "see" references on the health topic index pages.

▼ Testers commented about the lack of "news-breaking" health information. Others requested more popular features such as chat rooms, ask-a-doctor, body-fat calculators, etc. Since these usability tests have been concluded, a news wire service with the latest health news stories has been added to the site.

▼ Testers complained about overly technical information, in particular, the citations and abstracts found in the linked MEDLINE searches. Participants wanted information in language that they could understand - not too general but not so technical that they needed to consult a health professional for a translation.

▼ Users appeared less confused when links were distinctive from one another. Brief explanations or bulleted items under each link help ensure the user is following the right path and will find the expected and desired information.

In general, site design encompasses more than the "look" of the site. It is equally important to carefully monitor site links so that all URLs are valid. Server error (404) or "Sorry" pages should be customized to link back to the home page, a search page and/or a site map. Care should be taken to ensure the load time of all pages is reasonable on a variety of telecommunications connections.

NLM, a federal government organization, is mandated by law to ensure the site is accessible to all users. The site is tested on a variety of platforms, browsers (including a text browser) and browser versions, as well as screen reading and screen magnification software.

Conclusions about NLM's Experience with Usability Testing
General Tips for Usability Testing

There are a number of issues to be aware of when conducting usability tests with volunteers (both paid and unpaid). Testers often have no compelling reason to use your web site and answer the assigned tasks. Therefore, they are more likely to give up and become frustrated. There a number of things you can do to ensure valid test results and make it a favorable experience for the test participant.

▼ Don't overwork and exhaust the testers. If a tester is clearly confused and cannot complete the assigned task, move on to another task.
▼ Encourage testers to "think aloud" while they are performing the assigned tasks. Participant narration provides details on where and how problems arise, and allows testers to vent if they are frustrated.
▼ Clear web browser history between testers so highlighted links from tester to tester don't cause undue influence.
▼ The test administrator should not be part of the site development team. An administrator with neutral feelings about the site may be more willing to elicit honest feedback from the test participants.
▼ Users are poor designers, but good refiners. Don't expect your test participants to help design your site, after all, they weren't hired to do that. Users are good at spotting problems but generally don't have the knowledge necessary to design and build web sites.

Was Usability Assessment Worth It?

NLM's experience with usability assessment has been very positive, and we will continue to do testing on MEDLINEplus and our other NLM Web sites. Periodic heuristic evaluations by both national and local experts in the field of usability have alerted us to problems based on a set of defined heuristics. These heuristics include internal consistency, simple dialogue, shortcuts, minimizing the user's memory load, preventing errors, feedback and internal locus of control. As we add new resources to MEDLINEplus, we evaluate our design against these heuristic principles.

MEDLINEplus has also undergone focus group testing with senior adults. The testing quickly revealed areas in which all the participants had trouble. However, the group was sometimes "subverted" by the opinions of one or two more vocal participants. The testers who had no trouble with a particular site feature rarely voiced their pleasure, while the minority that had trouble tried to speak for the whole group. Useful information was gleaned from these focus group sessions, but caution should be exercised when solely relying on this method for evaluation.

Usability testing, of all the usability methodologies discussed in Chapter 1, has been the most beneficial for NLM. The testing has provided us a first-hand look at where and how users become confused on our site. It is not necessary to capture every usability testing session on video camera, but it does provide an explicit record of how users navigate and comprehend the site. Video taping readily enables future comparisons with other usability tests you may perform.

WORKS CITED

Cogdill, Keith. *MEDLINEplus Interface Evaluation: Final Report.* University of Maryland, Human-Computer Interaction Laboratory, August 1999.

CyberDialogue Inc. What Drives E-health Consumers to Sites? and Why Do They Stay?" *Cybercitizen Health Trend Report*, no. 20, 2000.

FURTHER INFORMATION

MEDLINEplus Interface Evaluation: Final Report. Keith Cogdill, University of Maryland, College of Library and Information Services and Human-Computer Interaction Laboratory. August 1999. Prepared for NLM.

MEDLINEplus Usability Test Report: December 1999. Sue G. Anderson, NLM internal document. March 2000.

Results of Usability Tests on the MEDLINEplus Web Site. Prepared b John Sorflaten, Human Factors International, Inc, in partnership with The Matthews Media Group, Inc. December 2000. Report prepared for NLM.

Review of MEDLINEplus Prototype Web Pages. William G. Cole, Information Design Seattle. March 2000. Report prepared for NLM.

So You Say You Want a Redesign: Usability, Accessibility and the Constraints of Designing a Database-Driven Web Site. Jennifer Marill, presentation given at the LITA National Forum 2000. URL: http://www.nlm.nih.gov/pubs/staffpubs/lo/litaforum/index.htm

National Library of Medicine: http://www.nlm.nih.gov
MEDLINEplus: http://medlineplus.gov

FOOTNOTE

1. For more information on the development and maintenance of MEDLINEplus, see Miller, Naomi, Eve-Marie Lacroix & Joyce E. B. Backus. "MEDLINEplus: building and maintaining the National Library of Medicine's consumer health Web service." *Bulletin of the Medical Library Association* 88(1) January 2000 (http://www.nlm.nih.gov/pubs/medlinepluspdf.pdf)

chapter 10

Walking the Web
Usability Testing of Navigational Pathways at the University of Nevada, Las Vegas Libraries
Jennifer Church, Jeanne Brown and Diane VanderPol

Background

The University of Nevada, Las Vegas (UNLV) is one of two public Universities in the state of Nevada. UNLV is an urban campus located in Las Vegas, a city of slightly more than one million people. The University's enrollment, staff and degree offerings have grown rapidly in recent years. UNLV offers 87 undergraduate and 75 Master's and Doctoral degree programs to approximately 23,000 students. The University Libraries are comprised of the Architecture Studies Library, the Curriculum Materials Library, a soon-to-be-opened Music Library, and the new 300,000 square foot state-of-the-art Lied Library, which is the main library.

The Study

A team appointed by the Dean of Libraries was charged with the re-design of the Libraries' web site to accompany the move of the main library into the new facility. The much-touted Lied building opening presented an opportunity to showcase library services and resources on-line as well as physically. Members of the re-design team and of the Libraries' Instruction Department chose to run a usability study to help inform the direction of this re-design effort.

We focused on the navigability of the site. Our objective was to gather and analyze data to better understand user navigational and organization tendencies in order to improve the Library web presence. We had the sense, through subjective observation, that much of the rich content of the library site was buried and not logically accessible to our users. We also believed that the information technology savvy of our student body, our largest primary user group, might need to be considered in redesign efforts. UNLV students possess a wide variety of experience with computers and the Internet. Information technology or computing competency requirements are decentralized and inconsistent from department to department. Students, depending on their major, may not be expected to be proficient users.

Study Methodology

We designed a survey instrument comprised of 20 questions. The questions asked participants to demonstrate information seeking behavior using the Library Website as a starting point. Surveys were administered on library computer workstations. The participant sat at the workstation and the individual administering the survey sat nearby observing the participant and noting their comments and actions.

The three library staff behind the usability study crafted the 20-question survey instrument (table 1). We tried to ask questions that mirrored the inquiries we hear at service desks and/or questions that directed participants to discover some of the web site's most important content.

We employed students to administer the usability surveys to reduce potential feelings of stress on the part of participants who might feel intimidated by library staff expertise. We did trial runs asking our student survey administrators to practice on new library staff. The trial runs helped us understand both how to better train the students to observe and annotate and also to adjust our questions for clarity. Two student employees did all of the survey administration.

We determined the number of volunteer participants in accordance with the Guidelines for OCLC's Usability Lab. The guidelines suggest that three to five participants will generally provide the needed information. We identified several types of users we hoped to gain information from and so decided to aim for approximately three to five users from each subgroup- undergraduates, graduates, and faculty- for a total of nine participants. The actual composition of the group was one faculty member, two graduate students and six undergraduate students.

Our campus has a Human Subjects Committee, which must approve any test, survey, questionnaire or experiment performed on campus. We were sure to report to the committee our plans and remain in compliance.

Initially, we sought volunteer participants through an open solicitation process. Signs were posted throughout the libraries and library staff mentioned it to potential participants they might know. Response was not particularly strong. We approached some faculty teaching undergraduate generalist courses and asked if they might be willing to encourage some of their students to help. Two professors offered students extra credit points for participation and the response was overwhelming. We took volunteer participants on a first come, first served basis until we had 6 undergraduated students scheduled. A library staff person took the calls and scheduled time for the participants

table 1. Web Usability
Study—Spring 2000

to meet with the students administering the survey. We allotted one hour for each participant to work at the 20 questions (three minute time limit per question) with an additional 15 minutes scheduled for preliminary instructions and filling out a release statement and an anonymous demographic survey.

Results:

Overall, the study revealed both structural and content problems within our site. As an added benefit, we gained useful insight into the general navigational tendencies of the participants. One consistent pattern worth noting was user preference for browser navigational tools (Home button, back button) over those incorporated into the site. Our internal navigational cues were located both at the top and the bottom of most pages. They were highly visible and defined clearly. However, time after time users chose the more familiar "Home" button on Netscape over the "UNLV Library Home Page" button

Can videos be checked out of the library? If yes, for how long?

Where is the Curriculum Materials Library (CML) located on campus?

Where would you go to look for online help using library resources?

Which online choices would you make to start the search for information on Buddhism?

Do the UNLV Libraries subscribe to the Journal of American History?

Where (on our site) could you find Internet resources for your biochemistry class?

Locate an article from yesterday's Las Vegas Review Journal.

What hours is Special Collections open?

Where would you find out about the newest books available at the Libraries on business topics?

How to do a citation in MLA format

Where would you look for full-text articles on the death penalty?

Where would you find out about the difference between a magazine and a scholarly journal?

What is the fine for overdue books?

Find directions for accessing the library's online indexes from home.

What is the name of the person in charge of Media Resources?

Where can you ask and submit an email reference question? (changed from "Where can you ask an online reference question?")

Submit an ILL request (also called Document Delivery) online or how can you request a book that library doesn't have from another library?

Where's an online dictionary?

What services are available for patrons with disabilities?

Where can you find links to government information online?

table 1. Web Usability Study—Spring 2000

present on each page. We attributed these patterns to user familiarity with the browser format.

Use and development of search tools:

Inexperienced users quickly turned to help and search tools that would, in essence, bring the desired information to them. We were surprised at the number of times participants turned to the site map, site index, help pages and site search engine. Several participants went directly to search tools for almost every question, without making an attempt to navigate the site in any other fashion. We did speculate that the time limits placed on the questions might have fostered this behavior by encouraging users to rush. The less practiced, undergraduate users were far more likely to engage in this type of search behavior than the more experienced users. Undergraduates averaged ten uses of a search aid per 20 question set while graduate/faculty users averaged only two. Interestingly enough, the browsing and link -following behaviors of the graduate/faculty participants were far more successful than the reliance on search tools exhibited by the undergraduate participants. The graduate student/faculty participants successfully answered 15 questions on average, while the undergraduate students averaged only 10 questions with successful outcomes.

On multiple occasions, participants employed search tool after search tool without success. This pattern revealed numerous weaknesses in our tools. One commonly used help feature consists of a series of pages titled "How do I...", "Where do I...", "Who is...", and "What is." In examining the results, it became clear that important content was actually missing. As an example, several participants went to the "How do I" section in order to discover how to request an item through Document Delivery. Although this was an apparently logical place to search, there was no entry for this task on the page. A close examination of these pages, as well as the glossary and site index, revealed that information was either incomplete or missing altogether. In order to address the overall development of these tools, a task force was formed from members of the various Public Service Departments. Its purpose was to redesign these help tools and expand their coverage.

Lack of necessary content presented itself in other ways, such as finding the locations of the libraries on campus. Although all nine participants uncovered the campus map in the help area, none could actually locate a specific branch on the map. Our old site linked directly to the University website's campus map. The individual branch libraries, located within certain departments, were not indicated on the map in any way. The solution was to design our own page that would highlight the libraries, rather than rely on the University site's current map.

Another difficulty occurred with our site search engine. It encompassed the entire University site with no method for restricting searches to the library web pages alone. Several participants voiced their frustration at the unrelated hits that resulted. This was corrected by adding a drop down feature to the search engine that allowed limiting the search to the library web site, to the University web site or to both. Conducting the same

figure 1. Navigation from
UNLV Libraries Home
Page 1999

searches as the students, we found this achieved a more manageable number of hits with the necessary information found within the first ten hits.

Buried content:

There was an overall hierarchical design to the site, which was organizationally sound. On occasion, however, navigating through it to find specific information presented unnecessary obstacles. The result was "buried content" that either required excessive navigation to find or went unused completely.

This concept became relevant in distinct ways. First, there was an overall lack of direct links from terms or items on the home page and the detailed information about those items. We did not incorporate enough shortcuts to allow users to go from page A to information on page D without first traversing pages B and C.

For instance, our old home page contained main headings with descriptors for items to be found under those headings (see figure 1). Those descriptors were not hotlinks nor did they extensively cover the information to be found. As a result, when our participants were asked to find out the library hours, they could not simply click on the phrase "library hours" on the front page. They had to click on "Library Information", then locate the "hours" section on that page and then click again before actually locating the information they needed.

Adding to this was the use of unclear, confusing terminology. "NEON Web", our name for the grouping of the catalog, indexes and databases and other research oriented information, had no meaning to the novice user. Even the descriptors underneath did not prove to be very illuminating. Using the term "databases" did not seem to indi-

figure 1. Navigation from UNLV Libraries Home Page 1999

figure 2. Navigation from the UNLV Libraries Home Page 2000

figure 2. Navigation from the UNLV Libraries Home Page 2000

cate to students that this was where they went to locate journal articles or find online newspapers.

In redesigning the site, we tried to eliminate as many "clicks" as possible between the user and the information they sought. In the redesigned front page, we eliminated the term "Neon Web", opting to call the main link to research sources "Research and Information." Additionally, we created mouseover menus that gave more detailed information on what was to be found in a given area and provided direct links to sub-areas (see figure 2).

We also attempted to clarify other cloudy terminology. "Databases" became "Find Journal Articles (Indexes)" and "Remote Access" became "Connecting from Off-campus"

Other important items were buried with very little to indicate they existed at all. As a result, these areas were seldom used. One of the most notable examples of this was our email reference service. Of the nine participants, only three were able to locate the page for submitting an email reference question. In our redesign, we put links to "Ask a Librarian" on the main help page and well as the Research and Information page that contains links to the catalog and databases.

In order to explore the overall impact of our changes, we studied page statistics from February 2000 (old site) and September 2000 (new site) to compare usage. These particular months were selected since both were second calendar months in a semester and had an equivalent number of overall hits (approximately 180,000 in the month). In February 2000, the reference email question page was accessed a total of 21 times. In

September 2000, after changing its prominence on the site, it was accessed 249 times. The Head of Reference, Shelly Heaton, reports that actual questions submitted have more than tripled since the redesign.

Another "buried" area was our link to Internet search tools. As noted earlier, several participants went immediately to Google and other search engines without using any internal search tools. Others attempted to use our tools, but left for external web engines after becoming frustrated with our site. In either circumstance, participants did not use the search engines links located within our own site to gain access to the web. This result was echoed by our web site statistics. The Internet search engine page was accessed only 24 times in February 2000. In redesigning the site, the Internet search page was included on the main Research and Information Page. The pages themselves were redesigned to allow users to use outside search engines directly from our site. They also include tips and tricks for using the search engines more effectively. Additionally, we now participate in a program with Google. The Google search places our library logo on the results page, encouraging users to return to our site when their search is complete. The results have been strong. In September 2000, users accessed these revised pages over 330 times.

Conclusions
Advice for others – recommendations and warnings.

The trial run of the testing proved to be an essential component in the process. It provided supervised experience for the student observers. The opportunity to try out and discuss recording requirements and techniques developed a joint awareness of the most important pieces of information and a consistent method for indicating those. In addition it served to identify questions that were unclear or misleading. It should be noted, however, that it did not weed out all of the misleading questions: during the study one question in particular proved to be so problematic that it was changed after the first two participants had failed to understand its thrust. The question originally read as " Where can you ask an online reference question?" Participants did not make the connection from this wording to email based services. The question was re-written as follows: "Where can you ask and submit an email reference question?"

The timed-question approach of the study, which included a maximum time limit for each question, had both advantages and possible consequences. The advantage of this approach is that we could indicate with some assurance the maximum time participants would need to allocate to the session. A possible consequence was that it may have encouraged a directed – as opposed to a browsing – solution to the questions posed. Asking for specific answers in a limited time may in fact account for the high use of search tools such as the search box and the help screens. Consequently we may have failed to identify behavior that occurs in a more relaxed situation.

Although we considered video or audio records of the sessions, we decided against this due to privacy issues, as well as the possible inhibiting effect. Not using such tech-

115

niques did have a downside however. The speed at which some users function as well as the complexity of some of the responses resulted in notes by the observers that were at times sketchy or confusing. Future studies will likely include some kind of automatic tracking component, possibly the Lotus screen tracking method.

Was it worth it? Would we do again?

During the course of the study we noted several general behaviors that were exhibited by more than one participant. These behaviors provided insight into how our web pages are used and accessed. Some of the observations are useful in improving our web site, and some have highlighted areas that Instruction can address in the future. There were of course many other observations related to our specific site and its organization.

Some of the general observations, based on both review of the results and comments of student observers include:

▼ Users are often not attentive to the URLs listed in search results. These clues are wasted opportunities for many.

▼ Users miss information that would have led to the answer or was itself the answer if that information is not highlighted or findable through a quick page scan.

▼ Certain non-library sites are chosen in preference to searching through library pages (e.g. yahoo.com and google.com). This may be because of patron familiarity with those pages, combined with their easy and memorable URLs.

▼ Patience is a trait that accounts for web navigational success fully as much as the organization of the site. Some users get close to the correct page but stop short. For instance, on one of the questions, one participant quit after trying three screens while another, for the same question, finally found the answer after seven screens.

▼ Users do search with search boxes and help screens. This result has energized library staff to enhance those search modes. What the behavior says about our information organization is not so encouraging, however, since search tools often seem to be used when menu choices do not clearly indicate the proper path. On the other hand, this may simply be a response to lack of familiarity with the site.

Timing of the study was an unforeseen factor in implementing changes based on what was observed. The study was conducted later in the semester than originally planned due to delays in obtaining funding and in recruiting student volunteers. This meant that results were obtained after the site re-design team was well into their task. Timing would conceivably have been more effective had the study been conducted prior to initiation of site re-design. Although some recommendations were implemented, the fact that this was done while we were in the midst of graphic re-design as well as re-constituting the top page meant that many suggestions had to be put aside, to be considered in the "next round" of web revision. This was exacerbated by the fact that the top page reconfiguration prompted the public services librarians to submit their own recommendations for site improvement.

We are committed to conducting the study again. The study was very useful in gaining insight into how our users approach the site. We are aware that we need to re-do the study to see if the changes that were made were actually improvements, and/or if the changes themselves created new gaps or problems. We know that unofficial comments from users about the site changes have been both positive and negative. We believe negative comments were due – at least partly – to a normal resistance-to-change factor. By allowing a semester to pass before conducting a second study with the new web design, we may minimize that factor's impact on assessing the new design and organization features. It will also allow time for patrons to familiarize themselves with the new layout.

Just as the web site is an ever-growing and changing work in progress, so too must observation of patron response to and use of the site be an on-going initiative.

University of Nevada, Las Vegas Libraries: http://www.library.unlv.edu, http://library.nevada.edu

José Aguiñaga holds an MLS from the University of Arizona in Tucson. He is currently an Academic Program Support Librarian at Arizona State University West, where he works with both faculty and student information needs. He chaired ASU West Library's Web Usability Team and helped design and administer the usability study described in this case study. José's e-mail address is jose.aguinaga@asu.edu.

Julie Bobay holds Master of Library Science and Master of Public Administration degrees from Indiana University. She is currently the Head of the School of Library and Information Science Library at Indiana University Bloomington, and holds the Walden Librarian position. Previously, as Head of the Electronic Resources and Services Team at Indiana University Bloomington Libraries, she led the redesign of the Libraries' web site; she served, with Mary Popp, as co-chair of the Working Group that assisted the consultants in their review of the Indiana University Bloomington web site. Julie's e-mail address is bobay@indiana.edu

Jeanne Brown is Head of the UNLV Architecture Studies Library. She has served on a series of library web design task forces, most recently the Web2000 team. She co-chairs the Libraries' Self-Assessment Committee.

Nicole Campbell holds an MLIS from the University of Michigan. She is currently a Reference Librarian at Washington State University Vancouver, where in addition to reference and instructional duties, she also serves as the library's Webmaster. Nicole has conducted usability studies of the library's Web site and presented on usability assessment with her colleagues at WSU. Information about her usability studies is available at: http://www.vancouver.wsu.edu/fac/diller/usability/website.htm. Nicole's email address is campbell@vancouver.wsu.edu.

Jennifer Church is the Head of the Information Commons in Lied Library at the University of Nevada, Las Vegas. She oversees a public computing area with workstations on all five floors of the building. The Information Commons provides productivity software and scanning to university students, faculty and staff.

Kathleen Collins holds an MLIS from Dalhousie University in Halifax, Nova Scotia, Canada. She is currently a Reference and Instructional Librarian at Odegaard Undergraduate Library at the University of Washington. Previously, she worked as an Academic Program Support Librarian at Arizona State University West, where she was a member of ASU West Library's Web Usability Team and helped design and administer the usability study described in this case study. Kathleen's e-mail address is collinsk@u.washington.edu.

Diane Dallis holds a Master of Library Science degree from Indiana University. She is currently the Instructional Design Librarian at the Undergraduate Library at Indiana University Bloomington. She served on the Working Group that assisted the consultants in their review of the Indiana University Bloomington web site. She also served as Interim Web Coordinator and led the "Task Force to improve the Search IUCAT/Database Page" that conducted usability studies to implement changes recommended in the consultants' reports. Diane's e-mail address is ddallis@indiana.edu.

William Gibbs is an Associate Professor and the Head of the Department of Media Services at Eastern Illinois University. He received his Ph.D. in Instructional Systems from The Pennsylvania State University. He has worked with individuals from various academic disciplines as part of instructional design teams and has served as instructional design and technology advisor to faculty in the development and evaluation of instruction programs.

Nicole Hennig is the Web Manager for the MIT Libraries. Her field of expertise is usable web design and usability testing, and she has spoken on this topic at conferences such as National Online and Internet Librarian. She also teaches a continuing education course on this topic at Simmons College Graduate School of Library & Information Science. Before coming to MIT in January of 1999, she was the Systems Librarian for Bose Corporation in Framingham, MA, where she designed and managed the home page for the corporate Intranet. She has worked in academic, corporate, and non-profit libraries for over 10 years and was formerly a classical musician, playing pipe organ and harpsichord in the Boston area.

David King is currently the Information Technology Librarian at Kansas City Public Library, and manages the library's public web site, the library staff's intranet, and a library consortium extranet. He has extensive experience in searching, creating and managing web sites.

Jennifer Marill is a Senior Systems Librarian with the Public Services Division of the National Library of Medicine. She is responsible for designing, building and maintaining MEDLINEplus, the Library's consumer health Web site. In addition, she manages the NLM public Web site and staff Intranet. Jennifer has spoken on and written about interface design, usability testing, web standards and integrated library system management. Jennifer's email is jennifer_marill@nlm.nih.gov.

Robert H. McDonald is the Web Development Librarian at the Auburn University Libraries. He holds an M.L.I.S. from the University of South Carolina - Columbia and an M.Mus. from the University of Georgia – Athens. He served as chair of the AU Libraries' Web Advisory Group during the course of this re-design project and administered and managed the usability testing described in this study. His Web site is http://www.auburn.edu/~mcdonrh and his e-mail address is mcdonrh@auburn.edu.

Gwendolyn Pershing holds a Master of Library Science from Indiana University. She is currently the Assistant Head of the Education Library at Indiana University. She has served on the World Wide Web Development Team. The Web Policy Committee and the "Task Force to improve the Search IUCAT/Database Page." Ms. Pershing has participated in usability studies of the IUCAT/Database page and of IUCAT, Indiana University Libraries on-line catalog. Gwen's e-mail address is pershing@indiana.edu

Mary Pagliero Popp holds Master of Library Science and Master of Science in Education degrees from Indiana University. She has been involved in academic library public services work and library instruction for more than 25 years and currently is the Library Information Technology Public Services Librarian at Indiana University Bloomington. She served, with Julie Bobay, as co-chair of the Working Group that assisted the consultants in their review of the Indiana University Bloomington web site. Mary's e-mail address is popp@indiana.edu.

Diane VanderPol is Head Instructional Services Librarian at the University of Nevada, Las Vegas. She has held that position for three years. Prior to moving to Nevada, she worked in college libraries in Michigan and North Carolina. She is a 1992 graduate of Syracuse University's Master's of Library Science program.

Suggested Web Sites and Readings

Useful Web Sites

HCI Bibliography: Human-Computer Interaction Publications and Resources – www.hcibib.org/

This site is maintained by Gary Perlman of OCLC and contains an extensive bibliography of print and Web materials that cover the field of human-computer interaction. Features include a news column and a search engine that is capable of searching all of the resources of the site.

IBM's Ease of Use Web Site – www.ibm.com/easy

This site previously called the IBM HCI Web Site is sponsored by IBM. It contains information for crafting Web sites that are user-friendly.

Usability First – www.usabilityfirst.com/

Contains information that makes Web sites and software easier to use including an extensive section on methods concerning usability evaluation.

Usable Web – http://usableweb.com

This Web site is maintained by Keith Instone, a Web usability consultant and information architect. It contains over one thousand links to usability-related Web sites. The links are arranged by topic.

Useit.com – www.useit.com

This is Jakob Nielsen's Web site. It contains many of his papers and the *Alertbox*, which are bi-weekly columns on the topic of usability.

Suggested Readings

Campbell, Nicole, Karen R. Diller and Janet Chisman. "Learning from Our Users: Usability Testing of WebPacs & Web Sites." *Proceedings of the Internet Librarian International 2000.* Medford, NJ: Information Today, 2000, pp 30-35.

Card, S.K., T.P. Moran and A. Newell. *The Psychology of Human-Computer Interaction.* Hillsdale, New Jersey: Lawrence Erlbaum Associates, 1983.

Chisman, Janet, Karen Diller & Sharon Walbridge. "Usability Testing: A Case Study." *College & Research Libraries,* 60:6 (November 1999) 552-69.

Corry, Michael D., Theodore W. Frick and Lisa Hansen. "User-Centered Design and Usability Testing of a Web Site: An Illustrative Case Study." *Educational Technology Research and Development (ETR&D),* 45(4), 1997: 65-76.

Dickstein, Ruth and Vicki Mills. "Usability Testing at the University of Arizona Library: How to Let the Users in on the Design." *Information Technology and Libraries*, 19(3), September 2000: 144-51.

Diller, Karen R. and Nicole Campbell. "Effective Library Web Sites: How to Ask Your Users What Will Work for Them." *Prepared for the Future: Proceedings of the Fourteenth IOLS '99*. Medford, NJ: Information Today, 1999, pp 41-54.

Dong, Jianming, and Shirley Martin. "Iterative Usage of Customer Satisfaction Surveys to Assess an Evolving Web Site." *Proceedings of the 6th Conference on Human Factors & the Web*, 2000: www.tri.sbc.com/hfweb/dong/hfweb2000.html

Dumas, Joseph and Janice Redish. *A Practical Guide to Usability Testing*. Norwood, NJ: Ablex, 1993.

Ericsson, K. A. & Simon, H. A. (1993). *Protocol analysis verbal reports as data*. Cambridge, Massachusetts: The MIT Press.

Ericsson, K., & Simon, H. A. (1984). *Protocol analysis verbal reports as data*. Cambridge, Massachusetts: The MIT Press.

Fichter, Darlene. "Head Start: Usability Testing Up Front." *Online*, January/February 2000, 79-81. www.onlineinc.com/onlinemag

Fowler, Susan. *Appendix B: Usability Tests*. www.fast-consulting.com/books/APPB.html

Frederickson-Mele, K., Michael D. Levi and Frederick G. Conrad. *Evaluating Web Site Structure: A Set of Techniques*. Bureau of Labor Statistics web site. http://stats.bls.gov/ore/htm%5Fpapers/st970070.htm

Fuccella, Jeanette and Jack Pizzolato. "Creating Web Site Designs Based on User Expectations and Feedback." IBM Corporation, Internetworking, June 1998, vol. 1.1, www.sandia.gov/itg/newsletter/june98/web_design.html

Gibbs, W.J. (2000). Media Services: Technology training initiatives. *Illinois Association for Educational Communications and Technology Journal*, Volume 5, 18-23.

Gibbs, W.J. & Shapiro, A.F. (1994). Video-split-screen technology: A data collection instrument. *Journal of Computing in Higher Education*, 5(2), 113-121.

Glitz, Beryl. "The focus group technique in library research: an introduction." *Bulletin of the Medical Library Association*, 85:4 (Oct 1997) 385-90.

Gordon, Seth. "User Testing: how to plan, execute, and report on a usability evaluation." *CNET Builder.com*, February 15, 2000. www.builder.com/Graphics/Evaluation/

Goulding, Anne. "Joking, being aggressive and shutting people up: The use of focus groups in LIS research." *Education for Information*, 15:4 (1997) 331-34.

Graphic, Visualization, & Usability Center. *Graphic, Visualization, & Usability Center's 10th WWW User Survey*. Georgia Institute of Technology web site. www.gvu.gatech.edu/user_surveys/survey-1998-10/

122

Hennig, Nicole. "Building a Database-Backed Web Site for E-Journals and Databases at the MIT Libraries: The Vera Project." Forthcoming in *Serials Librarian* (early 2002) and available at: www.hennigweb.com/publications/vera.html

Henninger, S. "A methodology and tools for applying context-specific usability guidelines to interface design." *Interacting with Computers*, 12, 2000: 225-43.

Hughes, Michael. "Rigor in Usability Testing." *Technical Communication*, Fourth Quarter 1999, 488-94.

Johnson, Robert R. User-Centered Technology: A Rhetorical Theory for Computers and other Mundane Artifacts. Albany, New York: Statue University of New York Press, 1998.

Karat, Claire-Marie. "Guaranteeing Rights for the User." *Communications of the ACM*, 41(12), 1998: 29-31.

Keinonen, Turkka. *Usability of Artefacts.* www.uiah.fi/projects/metodi/158.htm.

Levi, Michael D., and Frederick G. Conrad. *Usability Testing of World Wide Web Sites.* Bureau of Labor Statistics web site. http://stats.bls.gov/ore/htm_papers/st960150.htm

Massachusetts Institute of Technology. MIT Libraries Web Advisory Group. "Web Site Usability Test." (Documentation of usability studies conducted in March 1999). http://macfadden.mit.edu:9500/webgroup/usability/results/

Massachusetts Institute of Technology. MIT Libraries Web Advisory Group. "Card-sorting usability tests: the complete list of card names." http://macfadden.mit.edu:9500/webgroup/cards/cards.html

Massachusetts Institute of Technology. MIT Libraries Web Advisory Group. "Card-sorting usability tests: category survey." http://macfadden.mit.edu:9500/webgroup/cards/categories.html

Massachusetts Institute of Technology. MIT Libraries Web Advisory Group. "Card-sorting usability tests: reverse category survey." http://macfadden.mit.edu:9500/webgroup/cards/category-identification.html

Massachusetts Institute of Technology. MIT Libraries Web Advisory Group. "Card-sorting usability tests: detailed results." http://macfadden.mit.edu:9500/webgroup/cards/category2results.html

Massachusetts Institute of Technology. MIT Libraries Web Advisory Group. "Web site redesign process: http://macfadden.mit.edu:9500/webgroup/project.html

Massachusetts Institute of Technology. MIT Libraries Web Advisory Group. "Writing for the Web: Guidelines for MIT Libraries: http://macfadden.mit.edu:9500/webgroup/writing/

Morgan, Eric Lease. "Marketing Through Usability." *Computers in Libraries*, September 1999, 53-53.

Nakhleh, M. B., & Krajcik, J. S. (1991). *The use of videotape to analyze the correspondence between the verbal commentary of students and their actions when using different levels of instrumentation during laboratory activities.* Paper pre-

123

sented at the annual meeting of the National Association for Research in Science Teaching, Lake Geneva, WI.

Nemetz F., Winckler M. A. A., de Lima, J. V. *Evaluating evaluation methods for hypermedia applications.* ED-MEDIA & ED-TELECOM 97. 1997, Calgary - Canada.

Nielsen, Jakob. *Designing Web Usability.* Indianapolis: New Riders Publishing, 2000.

Nielsen, Jakob. "How Users Read on the Web." *Alertbox*, 10/1/97. www.useit.com/alertbox/9710.html.

Nielsen, Jakob. *Ten Usability Heuristics.* www.useit.com/papers/heuristic/heuristic_list.html.

Nielsen, Jakob. *Usability Engineering.* Boston: Academic Press, 1993.

Nielsen, Jakob. *The Use and Misuse of Focus Groups.* www.useit.com/papers/focusgroups.html.

Nielsen, Jakob & Darrell Sano. "SunWeb: user interface design for Sun Microsystem's internal Web." *Computer Networks and ISDN Systems*, 28:1-2 (1995) 179-88.

Norman, Donald A. *The Psychology of Everyday Things.* New York: Basic Books, 1988.

Otter, M. and H. Johnson. "Lost in hyperspace: metrics and mental models." *Interacting with Computers*, 13, 2000, 1-40.

Palmer, James E., et al. "The design and evaluation of online help for Unix EMACS: Access mechanisms." Human-computer interaction - *INTERACT '87: proceedings of the second IFIP Conference on Human-Computer Interaction.* Amsterdam: North-Holland, 1987; 461-66.

Palmer, et al. "Design and evaluation of online help for Unix EMACS: Capturing the user in menu design." *IEEE Transactions on Professional Communications.* 31:1 (1988) 44-51.

Pearsall, Susan H. "Web Design and Cognitive Clinical Interview." *Internetworking*, 3.2, 2000: www.internettg.org/newsletter/aug00/article_clinical.html

Pollock, Annabel and Andrew Hockley. "What's Wrong with Internet Searching." *D-Lib Magazine*, March 1997. www.dlib.org/dlib/march97/bt/03pollock.html.

Prown, Sarah. "Detecting 'Broke': Usability Testing of Library Web Sites." Yale University Library, 1999. www.library.yale.edu/~prowns/nebic/nebictalk.html

Reed, P., et al. "User interface guidelines and standards: progress, issues, and prospects." *Interacting with Computers*, 12(1999), 119-142.

Rubin, Jeffrey. *Handbook of Usability Testing: How to Plan, Design and Conduct Effective Tests.* New York: John Wiley & Sons, Inc., 1994.

Savage, RE. "Using a composite cognitive model for designing user-computer interfaces." *Proceedings of the 1986 IEEE International Conference on Systems: Man and Cybernetics.* New York, NY: IEEE, 1986; 435-38.

Sears, Andrew. "Introduction: Empirical Studies of WWW Usability." *International Journal of Human-Computer Interaction*, (12(2), 2000, 167-71.

Shneiderman, Ben, Don Byrd and W. Bruce Croft. "Clarifying Search: A User-Interface Framework for Text Searches." *D-Lib Magazine*, January 1997. www.dlib.org/dlib/january97/retrieval/01shneiderman.html.

Silipigni Connaway, Lynn, et al. "Online catalogs from the users' perspective: the use of focus group interviews." *College & Research Libraries*, 58:5 (September 1997) 403-20.

Smith, Pauline A. "Towards a practical measure of hypertext usability." *Interacting with Computers*, 8(4), 1996, 365-81.

Spool, Jared M. *Web Site Usability: A Designer's Guide.* San Francisco: Morgan Kaufmann Publishers, 1999.

University of Arizona Library. Access 2000 team page. (Includes presentations and documentation of usability studies conducted in 1997). http://dizzy.library.arizona.edu/library/teams/access9798/

Van House, Nancy A., et al. "User-Centered Iterative Design for Digital Libraries." *D-Lib Magazine*, February 1996. www.dlib.org/dlib/february96/02vanhouse.html.

Veldof, Jerilyn R., Michael J. Prasse and Victoria A. Mills. "Chauffeured by the User: Usability in the Electronic Library." *Journal of Library Administration*, 26(3-4), 1999: 115-40.

Wilson, Barbara Foley, and Margot Palmer. "Usability Testing of a Website and a Web user survey." *Proceedings of the Section on Survey Research Methods, American Statistical Association*, 1997: 1069-1073.